TOUCHING THE SURFACE

BY

ANDREW ROBERT DICKSON

Copyright © Andrew Robert Dickson 2009

All Rights Reserved.

The contents of this book may not be reproduced in any form,

except for short extracts for quotation or review,

without the written permission of the publisher.

ISBN: 978-0-9561598-0-9

Published by

Andrew Robert Dickson

Andrew@soul-evolution.com

www.soul-evolution.com

To Petra for being a wonderful Mum

To Oldriska for being a beautiful Daughter

Preface

- From everything you know, everything you see, everything you hear, every way you say, everything you think, everything you feel, everything you sense you become or duly created by you. The relevancies, influences, demands and restrictions all add up to you being you.

- Understood at a very young age I wondered why nobody is talking or even aware of what is happening inside. This book is a little bit of light on just that, an interpretation, understanding of being Human, from the inside, so that others can see and understand what they are also doing in their own way.

- Defining the elements and systems in brief, to what makes us a Human Being, from the Soul and Spiritual insights to the Practical and Scientific insights.

- Formulating this information has taken a lifetime just to comprehend a relevance of an understanding to an understanding that suits a Human. It is my version of the Human Being.

- Herein I can only share wisdom of an understanding for it is not for anyone to tell you yours. The attempt through the books is to give insight and understanding for a brief overview of what is Being Human.

- Therein the individuals reading the books take it upon themselves to do the same, share their inner knowledge of their own understanding of themselves and all that is apparent. Just communicate, have a chat about your understanding of the book.

- This book is a brief and not an exact guide, the detail is universally wide. There is immense amount of detail that makes up the brief, as it would just take to many lifetimes to formulate into words of relevance. Each time you read it (allowing a period to gestate); you gain more insight into your perception and understanding and relevancy of life.

- Call it a Table of Contents of Being Human or the Schematics, System Overview or a corporate structure of Being Human or the Cosmology Module of Being Human. It is an overview of the brief of the energy of Being Human. It is more so about the how you are you, in terms of energy than what you are.

Contents

Preface 4

   Contents *6*

Introduction 9

A Story of Human existence 12

Trend of Human Energy 16

Energy System – Soul 21

   Consciousness *22*

   Sub-Consciousness *22*

   Unconsciousness *23*

   Higher Consciousness *23*

   Overview *23*

Energy Perception 24

   Perceiving *24*

   Understanding Perception *26*

   Counter-Perception *34*

Soul-to-Soul Communications 35

   Densities of Perception *37*

Energies Layers and Trends 40

   Awareness *41*

   Observation *42*

Perception *42*

Belief *43*

Overview *43*

Energies Densities and Mass **44**

Understanding Emotional Densities *44*

Sadness (Anger or Hate) *48*

Happiness (Love or Peace) *57*

Relating Realities **66**

Life of Insights *67*

Deeper Meaning **96**

Understanding *96*

Self Understanding *97*

Depth of Insight *100*

Consciousness's *100*

Dimensions *101*

Modules - Tools *102*

Manifestations *103*

Abilities *103*

Influences *104*

Soul *106*

Filtering Desires and Inspirations *108*

Diagram 01 – Consciousness 110

Diagram 02 – Unconsciousness 112

Diagram 03 – Higher Consciousness 115

Diagram 04 – Emotions 118

Diagram 05 – Senses 120

Diagram 06 – Reality 122

Insights - Future Being **126**

Introduction

Advice when reading this book, generally you try to get into the authors frame of mind, I ask not to do this but read the words and focus on yourself, your mind, your thoughts, your feelings as if the book is acting as a guide to show you within you. Additionally expand this when not reading this book to everyday life whereby noticing the same, your awareness of, your perception of, your belief, and your comprehension.

Someone just implanted these schematics to Being Human in my head. Ouch! Now go and relate current knowledge, reality, and understanding, to these schematics, diagrams, procedures, overviews. My whole life has been about Understanding Being Human, the last 5 years has been about how to explain it consciously. This is the brief or just Touching the Surface.

The paragraph above is what now felt happened at the time it was immensely bewildering, did not have a clue what was going on. Went to work, went home, went drinking, got home, had some sleep, and started the process again the following day. That is what was going on. Slowly started getting weird insights, uncommon senses, and emotions, had good thoughts, but also bad thoughts, extremely bad, scary. It was like being inside everyone's consciousness, different characters, different perceptions, different beliefs, different observations, and different awareness's.

Just thinking these things does not explain it; it felt like that particular consciousness was inside. I would become the thought or the person or the emotion or sense or energy of what it was (not physically). Whether it would be a chat, conversation, a tree, a plant, the planet, or universe, economics, politics, architecture or design, forms or geometrics and so on, anything I could be aware of really.

With all this going on there was a very inwardly focused person. Focusing on comprehending all the immense movements happening, would look at every situation in every plausible or implausible way. I would look at it from a perception of anger, love, happiness, joy, hate, fear, calmness. Some would change my thoughts towards it, some would change my emotions about it, and some would change my senses regarding it.

Slowly but surely started getting a grasp on each aspect happening, otherwise I could eventually ended up in an asylum or prison. Would not recommend this approach to learn about consciousnesses, would take a slower process of change or adjustment next lifetime.

The interesting thing behind it all was this growing understanding happening, the overview of all these parts coming together about life, Being Human.

Five years later and still doing the same thing, there is a lot of knowledge known on the planet and the need to be aware of the knowledge known. To gain insight of history and the future in terms of how trends change, do your job better or live your life well. Seeing a reality of what and how is adjusting or changed towards its future.

Need to relate the understanding to common understanding. This is about shifting consciousness. Consciousness is an understanding of these books as it is only with consciousness that the books exist. The collaboration of all your conscious layers is the Soul. Simply put we are makeup of energy working with energy, and we as energy govern, manage and maintain our energy.

We have a linear and limited understanding of consciousness because of how we use it. Consciousness is relevant to everything we are as Human Beings. How we are aware of things, how we observe this and that, how we perceive and believe things.

This is why the books can only be an understanding, but in writing the books creates its own object for others to relate their understanding too.

Started writing a Journal October 2004 for insights mainly, very bespoke and difficult to understand reading it for the first time. Does show a wide and varied approach, insights to what was going on inside, see: Life of Insights?

To understand more than you currently know, you must adhere to knowing more than you currently understand. To know more than you currently understand you must adhere to understanding more than you currently know. It is cyclical, goes round and round like moon cycles. However, the intensity you perceive is important, either lighter more insightful, denser less insightful.

When asked how to understand this? I reply, I do not I am it; I accept it then evolve onwards. When asked how to know this I reply, I do not I am it, I accept it, then evolve onwards. In every moment, there is the answer and question to all that is relevant to understand or know. Further digression is just about different layers, directions of comprehension or perceptions each Human Being consciously relates to it. It is it, so understand.

Do not try to understand the book but allow and use it to show you your understanding of everything. Read it from your perception of your emotions, focus on your emotions while reading it. Read it from your perception of your thoughts, focus on your thoughts while reading it. Read it from your perception of your words, focus on your words while reading it. Read it from your perception of your senses, focus on your senses while reading it. Read it from your perception of design, focus on design while reading it. Read it from your perception of vibrations, focus on vibrations while reading it. Read it from your perception of understanding business, focus on business while reading it. Read it from your perception of understanding nature, focus on nature while reading it. The focused intent will cause you to relate to your desired type of understanding of your knowledge of something, like business, health, wealth, happiness, nature, and planet. Enjoy!

A Story of Human existence

This is the story of a being that is one of the most evolved souls ever perceived, coming of age to suggest changes to this reality. The knowledge known understood and comprehended within; to share is a manifestation of part of the knowledge to filter through like technology called Humanity.

The start happens trillions of years ago where a being of light came to know the essence of self on show. Developed over time a reality to be, full of advanced technology called Humanity. The beings are the same as the Universe as self is part of universe.

The working environment must be set in place for a self-regulating system within the universe. The world manifested as part of this team of energy modules sustaining and integrating with the universal energies. Energy moves and resonates to created the densities to manifestations and create the elements within the world within space. There are layers you see that energy runs through each layer getting denser until densities align to a current reality.

Nature is in charge of the elements to sustain the energy fields of a planet. Masses of energy filters through layers to become denser matter so organically and dynamically are renewed. The energy is constant to continuously be updating and sustaining with new information from the universe.

Life forms introduced to be freely living and in doing so moving and working to sustain themselves. Forms are a manifestation like legs, arms, body, and face. The energy forms though within these Humans that is, need to function and adapt dynamically. Let the Humans decide on what they need as they are a creation of themselves to use all the resources universally that they perceive. As in one layer, it filters through to the denser layers to be and reviewed and used. Each layer has protection or physics not to interfere but filter through understanding of action, events to other layers.

The energy modules called Souls, universally are training, evolving and integrate into Human form or body. This way they can intend the means of what they choose in there freely living surroundings and environment. All already known, as a Soul is to be with every movement of energy universally a restriction of dimensions shall apply to prevent the awareness from layers of densities to create from a position layered onwards from that moment integrated within the body. The restriction will work as a range so that the extent of depth will be that of two layers of conscious energy filtering within.

The freewill then applies within the scope of this range. This way they can freely be moving with denser energies filtered through the Human bodies aligned with their choice of reality determined by Human actions or interactions. Assisting with the lack of insight, all surrounding energies will service the needs of those restricted, by this we mean that if asked to provide something of service to Humanity the energies will filter through and provide if requested the directional understanding or guidance that Human beings need.

Thousands of years before now, they came to know that the essence of what they are is universal energy. The life they live always balancing with all that exists, being the job or work to do this. As energy moves universally about the elements within a Human, dynamically by choice of re-balancing, changes all energy that is around. Duly as a Human being will do, what it deems it needs the universal energy adjusts accordingly.

The matter of streams is relevant here to explain the extent of distance perceived from there to here. The energy filters through with movement then within the vibrations caused, effect structures and forms. Created from Humanity, duly within again the thought forms and methods sustain, and become reality; we perceive the words and physical actions are an intended need.

The journey of a being now in Human form is half way through life without knowing what it is he was prior to this life of strife. As the focus of the being is in a layer of words and actions, the extent of depth of awareness only goes as far as emotional relevance, albeit he is managing the rest but the conscious restrictions are in effect. However, something is different there is no restriction to the extent that he perceives. How does this man perceive the daily life of his Humanity and be.

The journey of the self is an interesting one to begin at a College in London, the 12 keys decoding the 12 knowledge is of reality. The key bearers by insight power the direction of the planet. The 13th knowledge guides realities. Set within the energy of the universe is the knowledge's of everything that is whether we become loving, hateful, fearful, angry, kindness; compassionate, empathic through our life is our choice. The 13th bearer is the sum of all the 12 as a prime interface for direction of the planet. Long ago in a reality, way before the present, a soul with energy that had decoded information on how to heal the planet, to protect the planet, the energy encoded with 12 souls has to decipher instructions to heal the planet when all 12 become one again. Hidden within all lifetimes was the essence of what comes about today.

To journey through lifetimes, with the trials and tribulations to be ever present as the 13th bearer. The journey involves the single mum, the politician, the technician, the scientist, the artist, the king, the cleaner, the banker, the architect, the gardener, the sportsman, and the mechanic. The present day involves the retracing and finding of the soul's that hold the keys of knowledge, to bring together as one. Other aspects involve Wizardry, Magic, Beings, Dragons, Fairies, Angels, Elementals, Demons, Warlocks, Witches, Humans, Death, Destruction, Harmony, and Peace.

Combining all that is good and bad all that is ok and sad. To ascend this reality you must first learn to live in this reality the parts of reality, the harmful, the loving, the caring, the hurtful, the supportive, and the destructive. Once the lifetimes have past and the being can exist in each of all the realms of knowledge they can ascend with full knowledge of where they are ascending. The neutral reality that influences and applies energy to all aspects of the current is reality. No harm can affect the beings of neutral reality. All matter exists within all realities.

Stories of Love, Stories of Compassion, Stories of Destruction, Stories of Harm and Anger, Stories of Action, Stories of Adventure, Stories of Myth and Magic, Stories of Competition and Excellence, Stories of Elegance and Grace, Stories of Manipulation, Stories of Drama all become in part the whole. The power keys are power to influence awareness, power to influence perception, power to influence consciousness, power to influence thoughts, power to influence words, power to influence belief, ability to fly, ability to teleport, ability to move objects, ability to be invisible, ability of telepathy, ability of healing. Each incarnation he does not know the previous abilities or powers, he needs to work out each time and see what else he can obtain.

Suspense while all this is going on and others are on the same journey to inspire their intent of the world onto the populace for their gain. As the previous incarnation influences his next there is a period of living the way he did without understanding why, changing his/her intent of self, mannerism to the existing reality, and finding the keys.

Trend of Human Energy

Long, long ago in a time unknown a society roamed with elegance and grace as they go. The life was bliss and all things possible without restriction of that and this. It all began with a group of beings where their insights of self-sustaining a resonance that fill them with joy and happiness in anything they did was managed by them as each understood what they did. Wanting to help others attain their understanding that they had gained started sharing the inner belief and abilities that others seek for their own.

Understanding the dos and don'ts to what affects them, they begin building a society based on their knowledge of each. Everyone was party to the plan and understood the need, all was part of this, shared in their comprehension to sustain and build it. There fundamental technology was that energy from the planet filters through them and they filter and direct in such a way that fulfils the essence inside them everyday this then grew, as energy would continuously filter through to become a more powerful and stronger reality that they view. Because development was so fast, they soon learned to let go of the old view and run with the forward to bring about the new, so the energy would fill and fill what existed to become greater and grander than the situation before.

Not long before, it grew and more and more people knew that this society and way of living was so great and beautiful they all came along to see and be in this reality. Hundreds of years have passed and the essence of all interlinked to this presence of each individual giving weight to all the aspects that each individual would be grateful. Life amazingly fulfilled and no other requests or needs were desire apart from sustaining this wonderful continent.

There came a time where they would get used to being in it all that other ideas would be beneficial. Whereby the current society would link all thoughts and views and share in the knowledge to create the prime overall view, there becomes other opinions that individually they would become better off if they went their own way instead of this whole one. Energy was vast and used freely to move and create each opinion and view.

The desires where shared like a virus in their heads would creep in and each individual would sustain in part an opinion of this view that each individual would benefit from this way not the all. As before and as designed the energy would fulfil the desire to enhance the views individually and so it grew. Desire became to be a view that each individual will benefit from, there starts a growth where some will lead, and others follow with just their belief.

The directions of each individual are collaborated and strongest belief took the reins and led. The direction they took was to sustain a belief that they would each be better off if they went their way. Time went passed repeatedly and the essence of what was creating, integrated within each individuals view was this element of a desire to be individual. Hundreds more years have passed by this way and the individuals views and desires took play, their actions are now taking hold of their view their inner desire to be individually beneficial. A structure started and hierarchy formed, people would follow and train when born, that this way is better for you than a wholly united equal form.

Energy was continuously fulfilling the requests that soon almost everyone have made a desire to be individually fulfilled with the only belief, which by now was adhering to the structures belief's. They directed there energy to move this way into a structure that would feed more energy to others in multiple of ways. It was not long before they knew that their energy was mostly enhancing others but not them in this structure built by them.

Where is the abundance that we had before we seem to be limited in the energy that we had. More and more energy would filter through with their intents and belief for the individual view. The energy sustaining and growing the structure in place each individual would have his or her own place. Potency was increasing with dissatisfaction of each whereby they would lead this structure and the others would hesitate. Leaving the united form for the structured view became the balance of society where one would be this view and the other would be that view.

Energy was still filtering both desires through to each of the forms structurally in view. The structure was building individual's energy at the top and the lower structural plains would have less to use. Led by their belief and there structure to be they were led to get more people and energy. The desires of the individuals leading the hierarchy view wanted more energy to do what they wanted to do, as in their way they were happier. Stronger and stronger they felt they could be that they fought for their desire with people led by them. The harshness of energy used this way caused immense hurt and much pain.

The leaders that led that energy to this day are still doing the same in this society this way. Thousands of years have passed by and more and more energy streamed to sustain this desire and view to exist this way in the structured view. Although a structure existed before, the whole of the structure moved, as the energy balanced and shared across the relevancies of the desires in each individuals care.

A war begun unlike anything anyone had seen before where pushing and demanding became part of the structured view to obtain and sustain the individual from being who he or she needs to be in his or her view. Because of the amount of energy filtered through no one could remember how this all started they just knew what they individually followed, to do either by leading or following they desire to be. Now the structure is gaining weight without understanding of how it came to be this way. The unified view became less and less as the best options presented for the individual to become better than before was to follow the structure than balancing out the energy filtering through each individual.

As the people became only trusted in themselves segmentation started to build, as the rich of energy filter through the populace and knew the remaining populace became bemused as the energy towards sharing was being unused. So less and less sharing, more, and more of personal views became stronger in the structured individual. Objects were a way of saying that this effort is worth this object for what you as an individual do but they already received energy filtering through.

The leaders worked out that if the populace could stream all their energy to their means they would become greater and grander with energy that filters through as each individual is giving weight to this view. The structures in place people follow this with pace, to obtain which is personally something of a benefit to individuals. This would continue overtime whereby no one then knew why he or she would be filtering and using the energy through them to the hierarchy in place and being directed to the leaders in place.

Something was brewing that would start to degrade the energy that was filtering through this way; the energy from the planet that was filtering through was reducing in potency because of what was being used. Less and less desires and views were of environment and surrounding against the individuals desire for the individuals view. Thousands of years would pass this way, degrading the energy from the planet each day, caused by the individuals to see only their individual desire in each of them for themselves. Feeding all the energy to filter through the hierarchy to maintain, sustain the structure in place.

Objects and buildings became the segmented growth whereby more focus to the external development of using the energy from all to see only what is in front and follow the lead. As so, the energy filtered this way to sustain and grow the elements of what each individual gives weight to know. So many objects and external tasks to be done that no longer does anyone look towards the essence coming through but where to use it and sustain it from the structured hierarchy in view. Some would challenge this way to be as they long for their old desire to share and be freer, but put in their place was this structured society, as it does not conform to the essence of all energy filters through to the hierarchy.

The growth continues and great many things of desire created for use by all that follows the structured tree and more density created by filtering the energy to each object or building. The density becomes stagnant and does not adjust like the human beings creating through time their way. Objects of density can only be and the energy filters to it all the while the builders and users need.

At a time, not so far away the intensity of need for more would potently be the direction of all the structures in societies. Different structures overtime and more people filtered their energy and directed to their leaders they became the essence of what was in line to hierarchy they believe to become greater than they currently be. Dominance and rule of all became the journey for the structured individual societies. Led by one and followed by all perceived that this was the way to fulfil that same inner desire, that once was and is still within the depth of energy within them all. Consciousness no longer has an understanding known, but what is within the self to show. Therefore, the journey of life this day this way is to follow the majority as it flows its way. Led by leaders that leading is their own way, rather than release the energy to balance and share in every way.

The destruction of many lives and objects on route have since made an impact to turn a new where the essence of once was is now coming through but the structure remains as yet unchanged. Individuals are becoming more understanding to what is within than is external so the journey reverses itself to balance. During the phase of building the structure for a few, that benefit from the openness from the earthly or planetary view. The energy that once was so immensely fine is only a fraction now as it once was in the sky. We give little credit to what filters through that sustain us in health, wealth, and happiness to renew. We are not the buildings that stand rigid and solid but are the changing dynamic of organic. All of our imperfections come through as it is from ourselves to be, as we individually desire our need.

The balancing of all the planetary energy is to be the most adventurous journey ever. Re-aligning our thoughts and feelings too that balance of sharing and combining the essence of all in each of you. Yet comes to the belief of each of us we forever stuck in our inner building blocks from history. The energy still runs through us the way that it did and we can rebuild by creating again the bliss. This in turn releases from the need for densities or harshness within. As before, it is again and takes time to build and sustain. The journey is long and arduous too where all the effort is about that focused view.

Energy System – Soul

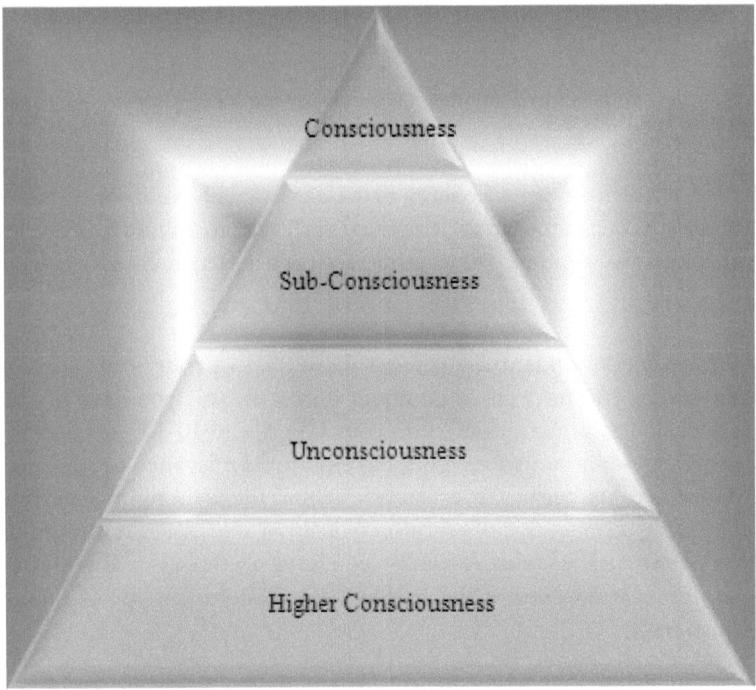

A linear perception, Soul and Consciousness layers.

Consciousness

Consciousness is the part of the immediate, the present, and the moment. All that is necessary for your consciousness is to identify existence or acceptance. Consciousness uses your Sub-consciousness as a means of memory and trends (a cache of conscious relativity) to calibrate what or how you wish to proceed with a thought, emotion, and sense. Keeping the existing sub-conscious trend of sense, emotions, thought, or change it.

The consciousness is used constantly but limited in its soul usage (10-15%) in depth or broadness that it can achieve. It is just energy, to expand your conscious relativity to things, conversations or objects just perceive more of it in that moment, but focus inwardly. You are consciously creating and manipulating trends of your sub-consciousness.

Consciously we project our focus external from ourselves a lot more than internally, to ourselves, so the result being we give less focus to what is apparent sub-consciously and more to what is apparent externally like, a job, a person, a society, a group, a country, a task, a chat.

Sub-Consciousness

The trends of types of energy that co-exists with your consciousness, then consciously you can just focus on what is relevant to you now. You have millions of trends that require you to think, feel, sense, act, and move while consciously going about your moment of whatever you need to do.

The sub-conscious usage is huge about 85% of your Soul is made up of routines and trends you have set to go about things the way you have perceived them best consciously at that moment in your life. About 10-15% of that is consciousness. Sub-consciousness has a big emotional relevance to sub-conscious trends in today's reality because it exists just behind those thoughts consciously, focus and become more aware of emotional detail or relevance. Without thoughts you still have emotions, without emotions you have no thoughts. Energy streams through your emotions to create and sustain your thoughts or type of thoughts you had chosen to have.

On a spiritual note, your sub-conscious ascends from within your Soul through to your consciousness. The structure of your thinking, the form of your thoughts, the manner in which you speak, the attitude you use. All stored as energy, like a database. Consciously you are interacting with your sub-conscious or should say a bit of your consciousness each time you use it, a bit of memory or knowledge you already know, how you talk, how you think. You are increasing your capacity or reforming it each time you are thinking or knowing about something you do not know, to evolve the Soul. Amazing technology, we are.

Unconsciousness

Unconsciousness is the holding or magnetising of the energy that includes your sub-consciousness and duly consciousness. Like the playing field or plot of land where something could be created. It is also the spiritual position known as embodiment, the whole self, being one with the Universe.

The energy on this plateau is incredible; it is where a dream is real and reality is a dream. What you create from here is your resonance that acts as a structure to your sub-consciousness to which defines stability in your design or how you are as a person, what you need to interact with, it's the, you bit, in being one with the Universe.

Higher Consciousness

The interaction and influences from the elements of the energy across the planet and/or Universe. As any energy changes or moves in the Universe, within you or other side of the planet, energy influences you and your approach to that influence is about your position in the grander scheme of things, planetary wide. We are all about the energy. Depending where you are at or positioned consciously in dimensions you act in accordance to your position. It is like having a job and receiving a complex email that you are capable of doing or is your job function. Duly you then deal with that email or energy in the case of consciousness or sub-consciousness.

Overview

Consciousness is everything you know, known and are about to know. The trend of progression on how energy evolves, and you evolve. It is the fabric of everything sustaining life, as we know it but in our own individual way. It is knowledge and understanding, how you use it and identify with it defines you as being human.

Energy Perception

Comprehending and perceiving are almost the same, comprehension seems more defined, and perception is more work in progress, not conclusive yet. Comprehending is the defining of belief.

Perceiving

We are the construct of a system of Energy, Light, and Matter (Densities of matter/mass). Different varying degrees of matter (in terms of density of matter), working in infinite number of ways and forms, what our senses, emotions, thoughts, words are. Do not believe me, Believe in yourself, but it takes you to look. Everything is relevant whether it be Spiritual or Science, being Normal, being Human.

The Billions of bits of information, or energy we decipher or read in a day is incredible. Respect and appreciation to what we have in our way of understanding. Then again, so much more understood individually and growth of us will progress quicker. Life is inclusive of Life, Life sustains Life. How we go about our tasks and issues becomes the foundation of how we live our lives.

Just like a Computer System (although much more advanced), trends and routines are a major part of life's motions, movements, or automated processes. Your mind is a construct of your life's interactions, not just physically. The relevancies, circumstances, the routines, the methods, the attitudes associated, the manners, best practices. The process of changing what makes you, is the reverse, change the way you act towards something and that something becomes (to you) your new way, do it regularly and it becomes routine.

We are just energy moving with energy in directions of light or focus creating or releasing densities of energy or matter. The relevancy to us is the lighter the matter the more understanding and broadness; the less pressure on our consciousness builds up.

The words you use see how they define you, harmfully in expression or harsh, dense in manner. Other way is the lighter side of matter being gentle, softer in expression, or more towards angelic. The degrees of density of words for expression are paramount to see how you currently allow yourself or push yourself. It is all just energy forcefully creating stronger mannerism or expression is creating denser energy as it takes more energy to create words of a denser degree than you currently sustain as yourself. Different people, different degrees of density, but the method is the same. The lighter more gentle approach uses less energy to create, as it is lighter density, it is reducing density of matter. The types of words are not as important as the mode of the expression of words.

Actions change dependant on your ability to change the manner or attitude of your physical self. Through your life the manner and attitude, you have taken towards everything builds up into a database or cache of relevancies (subconscious) of how you go about life. How you use your words has relevancy to how you align with you and your surroundings.

Understanding Perception

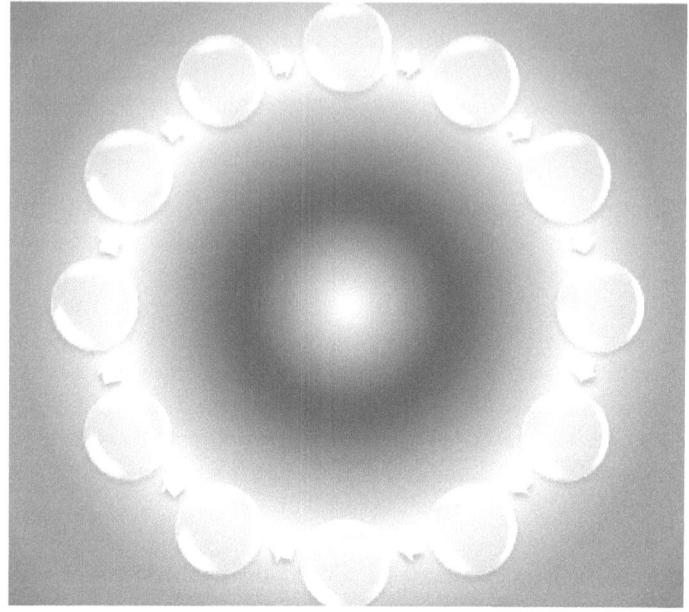

- Honour
- Respect
- Observation
- Perception
- Understand
- Acceptance
- Comprehend
- Ascend
- Package
- Release
- Cleanse
- Balance

The Rainbow coloured background is relevant to the Soul at Emotional level or density.

- **Honour** – How you honour something, someone is how you as energy are honouring something as energy. Change the way you honour it to enhance or evolve the energy of it, say honouring it brighter or lighter, more pleasantly, more harmoniously than before.
- **Respect** - How you respect something, someone is how you as energy are respecting something as energy. Change the way you respect it to enhance or evolve the energy of it, say respecting it brighter or lighter, more pleasantly, more harmoniously than before.
- **Observation** - How you observe something, someone is how you as energy are observing something as energy. Change the way you observe it to enhance or evolve the energy of it, say observe it brighter or lighter, more pleasantly, more harmoniously than before.
- **Perception** - How you perceive something, someone is how you as energy perceive something as energy. Change the way you perceive it to enhance or evolve the energy of it, say perceiving it brighter or lighter, more pleasantly, more harmoniously than before.
- **Understand** - How you understand something, someone is how you as energy understand something as energy. Change the way you understand it to enhance or evolve the energy of it, say understand it brighter or lighter, more pleasantly, more harmoniously than before.
- **Acceptance** - How you accept something, someone is how you as energy accept something as energy. Change the way you accept it to enhance or evolve the energy of it, say accepting it as brighter or lighter, more pleasantly, more harmoniously than before.
- **Comprehend** - How you comprehend something, someone is how you as energy comprehend something as energy. Change the way you comprehend it to enhance or evolve the energy of it, say comprehend it as brighter or lighter, more pleasantly, more harmoniously than before.
- **Ascend** - How you ascend something, someone is how you as energy ascend something as energy. Change the way you ascend it to enhance or evolve the energy of it, say ascending it as brighter or lighter, more pleasantly, more harmoniously than before.

- **Package** - How you package something, someone is how you as energy packaging something as energy. Change the way you package it to enhance or evolve the energy of it, say package it as brighter or lighter, more pleasantly, more harmoniously than before.
- **Release** - How you release something, someone is how you as energy release something as energy. Change the way you release it to enhance or evolve the energy of it, say releasing it as brighter or lighter, more pleasantly, more harmoniously than before.
- **Cleanse** - How you cleanse something, someone is how you as energy cleanse something as energy. Change the way you cleanse it to enhance or evolve the energy of it, say cleansing it as brighter or lighter, more pleasantly, more harmoniously than before.
- **Balance** - How you balance something, someone is how you as energy balance something as energy. Change the way you balance it to enhance or evolve the energy of it, say balancing it as brighter or lighter, more pleasantly, more harmoniously than before.

These represented as the 12 circles regulating your conscious balance and understanding, or alignment. They are also represented as the planetary energy portals which in-turn the planet regulates its consciousness in the same regard.

Billions of bits of energy run through you daily allowing you to sense, feel, think, walk, talk, see, and hear in multiple ways that you choose. The energy looks after your mind, body, and spirit.

That energy is also dynamic, dimensional, systematic, neutral, and harmless. Aches and Pains, emotional or stressful issues are just denser pressure of energy than you care to handle. We consciously interact with it to think this or that, do this or that but we do not consciously realise we are interacting with it. Our sub-conscious takes care of that by trends and routines we have decided upon through our life. Unconsciously interacts with influences and adjustments with external energy by means of our higher consciousness.

So energy is filtering or running through various conscious layers daily to be able to do what we do, say what we say, think what we think, feel what we feel, and sense what we sense. As energy runs through layers of us, it becomes denser as it keeps filling up inside us until we let it out, exertion or talking, or shouting or expressing thoughts, or expressing feelings, or expressing senses. The energy needs to run through us to sustain the density we hold our consciousness at, this by means of our perception of reality, what we associate to, what we want or need.

The systematic guide at this level is to keep things simple but to the point. As energy gets denser it becomes more defined and harsh, due to more and more energy is required to build that density.

Harsh words or thoughts created by increasing energy to that thought or word you are trying to express. Your perception learns from you so if your perception is at a dense layer of your consciousness you will perceive and act at that layer of density or harshness.

I say dense as in denser than your normal density, or layer of density.

Conscious Perception Level 2-3

- Linear Perception
- Physically hard
- Harsh physical action
- Harsh thoughts
- High Intensity
- High Pressure

In the subtitle, "linear perception" relates to perceiving things as very defined, to the point, strong and hard.

In the subtitle, "physically hard" relates to perceiving people or want people to define themselves, to the point, strong and hard.

In the subtitle, "harsh physical actions" relates to physical manner as you walk or talk, stamping on the ground as you walk, pressurising and demanding as you talk, strong and hard.

In the subtitle, "harsh thoughts" relates to manner of thinking as you think or digress, pressurising and demanding as you think, strong and dense.

In the subtitle, "high intensity" relates to attitude of action as you think or digress, pressurising and demanding as you push your will outwardly towards someone or something.

In the subtitle, "high pressure" relates to attitude of action as you think or digress, pressurising and demanding as you maintain pressure of your will outwardly towards someone or something.

Conscious Perception Level 3-4

- Multi-Linear Perception
- Physically soft
- Soft physical action
- Soft thoughts,
- Low Intensity
- Low Pressure

In the subtitle, "multi-linear perception" relates to perceiving things as slightly defined, multiple points, erratic and slightly weak.

In the subtitle, "physically soft" relates to perceiving people or want people not to define themselves and be open to other ideas, not so to the point, free and gentle.

In the subtitle, "soft physical actions" relates to physical manner as you walk or talk, gentle, elegance as you walk with no pressure, relaxed, as you talk, soft and gentle.

In the subtitle, "soft thoughts" relates to manner of thinking as you think or digress, hardly any pressure, and softly as you think, gentle and light.

In the subtitle, "low intensity" relates to attitude of action as you think or digress, low pressure and accepting as you drive your will gentle outwardly towards someone or something.

In the subtitle, "low pressure" relates to attitude of action as you think or digress, low pressure and no demands as you maintain course of your will outwardly towards words or physical.

Conscious Perception Level 4-5

- Dimensional Perception
- Physically light
- Light thoughts
- Light Emotions

- Light Resonance
- Light Pressure

In the subtitle, "dimensional perception" relates to perceiving things in multitude, multiple points, erratic and slightly disengaged.

In the subtitle, "physically light" relates to perceiving people or want people not to define them and be open to other ideas, not so to the point, free and light.

In the subtitle, "light thoughts" relates to mental manner as you walk or talk, gentle, elegance as you walk with no pressure, relaxed, as you talk, soft and gentle. Thinking in a light meditative state as you go about your way.

In the subtitle, "light emotions", relates to manner of feeling as you feel, light pressure, and softly as you go, gentle and light emotions.

In the subtitle, "light resonance," relates to attitude of action as you sense or communicate, light vibrations and loving as you row your will gentle outwardly towards someone or something.

In the subtitle, "light pressure", relates to attitude of action as you sense or resonate, light resonance and no demands as you maintain course of your desire outwardly towards thoughts or words.

Conscious Perception Level 5-6

- Multi-Dimensional Perception
- Physically angelical
- Enlightened thoughts
- Enlightened Emotions
- Soft Resonance
- Fractional Pressure

In the subtitle, "multi-dimensional perception" relates to perceiving multiple in multitude, multiple insights, erratic and slightly disengaged. Inwardly calm.

In the subtitle, "physically angelic" relates to perceiving people or accepting people are calm, relaxed and be open to other ideas, not so to the point, free and harmonic.

In the subtitle, "enlightened thoughts" relates to mental manner as you walk or talk, spiritual, resonant as you walk with no pressure, relaxed, as you talk, soft and gentle. Meditative states as you go about your way. Deep Insights

In the subtitle, "enlightened emotions", relates to manner of feeling as you feel, light resonance, and softly as you go, and light emotions hardly noticeable.

In the subtitle, "soft resonance," relates to attitude of action as you sense or communicate, light vibrations and loving as you row your will gentle outwardly towards someone or something. Harmonic, peaceful expressions and resonate through.

In the subtitle, "fractional pressure", hardly noticeable relates to attitude of action as you sense or resonate, light resonance and no demands as you maintain course of your desire towards emotions or thoughts.

Overview Perception

You will notice only a slight difference or adjustment at each Level as there is a very fine line between each of them. That fine line takes years to notice change normally. The reason it takes years is that you are not conscious over those changes in you; all changes for you are actions from your conscious awareness so that the energy system delivers energy to that conscious perception or your reality. The moment you become consciously aware, you can observe and perceive in multiple ways and make necessary adjustment to your mannerisms, attitudes, physical form, and your words.

When understanding try to only perceive your understanding then understand other peoples so you can consciously integrate their understanding with yours. The more you identify with your understanding, the more you will understand about theirs. It is much easier to do that consciously than not being aware you are doing it consciously.

Comprehensions

Perception level 2 you will identify with perceiving and believing in energy that is at that perception level and some of level 3. Anything outside that you will deny belief of, not want to know, choose to ignore it. This is because of your binding with your current reality. How you wish to exist in terms of density of the energy that runs through you. You will also understand level 1 and not pay it much attention because your understanding is greater, not as limited. Helping those of a denser level is a responsibility level 2 perceptions; because you consciously understand, level 1 comprehensions. It is your helping others to understand more towards your current understanding.

Perception level 3 you will identify with comprehending and believing in energy that is at that perception level and some of 4 and 2. Anything outside that will not be of interest, boring, or the other way interesting or desired. This is because of binding in this reality, what is common perception. You will also understand level 2 and not pay it much attention because your understanding is greater, not as restricted or limited. Helping those of a denser level is a responsibility level 3 perceptions; because you consciously understand, level 2 comprehensions. It is your helping others to understand more towards your current understanding. Your desired perceptions lead you more so towards level 4 perceptions.

Perception level 4 you will identify with comprehending and believing in energy that is at that perception level and some of 5 and 3. Anything outside that will not be of interest, but important, or the other way interesting and desired. This is because of binding in this reality, what is common perception. You will also understand level 3 and not pay it much attention because your understanding is greater, not as restricted or limited. Helping those of a denser level is a responsibility level 4 perceptions; because you consciously understand, level 3 comprehensions. It is your helping others to understand more towards your current understanding. Your desired perceptions lead you more so towards level 5 perceptions.

Perception level 5 you will identify with comprehending and believing in energy that is at that perception level and some of 6 and 4. Anything outside that will not be of interest, but important, or the other way interesting or desired. This is because of binding in this reality, what is common perception. You will also understand level 4 and not pay it much attention because your understanding is greater, not as restricted or limited. Helping those of a lesser level is a responsibility level 5 perceptions; because you consciously understand, level 4 comprehensions. It is your helping others to understand more towards your current understanding. Your desired perceptions lead you more so towards level 6 perceptions.

Perception level 6 you will identify with comprehending and believing in energy that is at that perception level and some of 7 and 5. Anything outside that will not be of interest, but important, or the other way interesting or desired. This is because of binding in this reality, what is common perception. You will also understand level 5 and not pay it much attention because your understanding is greater, not as restricted or limited. Helping those of a lesser level is a responsibility level 6 perceptions; because you consciously understand, level 5 comprehensions. It is your helping others to understand more towards your current understanding. Your desired perceptions lead you more so towards level 7 perceptions.

Counter-Perception

Following the perceptions and levels of above, perceive the opposites as if it was you or you were it. The relevancy of doing so increases your perception on any given object or person. When you perceive from the other side of your perception you identify inwardly within yourself what is perceivable within another object or person.

When talking with someone you act according to your perception of what you need to say and how you need to say it. Counter-perceiving gives you understanding from the other (person) where you understand how or why someone is saying and how he or she are saying it based on their own perception of understanding themselves. The counter-perception you understand you and identify how you would say that or how you would say this and development your own perception from a linear one-track perception to a multi-perceptional understanding.

The more you do it with as many mannerisms or attitudes you have and counter-perceive them the more you will develop your understanding of your perception so that when you counter-perceive you gain insight to others and understand them better. It is all just about the energy in this position or that position, or consciously perceiving this way or that way which in turn sets within your sub-conscious a trend or pattern of how you wish or desire to understand things or evolve yourself.

Notice differences in your perception, when your angry your perception of things or people is different to when you are happy. When you are sad, or hateful your perception is slightly different again. When you are in Love again your perception changes but you can use that perception whenever you wish, just keep developing and practicing using it in different ways and your learning curve will increase.

Remember it is about your understanding, as most others will pick a slightly different perception even though they may know they have other perceptions to choose. The point is being aware of your dynamic perception means you have the conscious choice rather than an unconscious one.

Soul-to-Soul Communications

Understanding of your Senses gives you greater Understanding of the senses of others. Understanding of your Emotions gives you greater Understanding of the emotions of others. Understanding of your Thoughts gives you greater Understanding of the thoughts of others. Understanding of your Words gives you greater Understanding of the words of others.

Any conversation happens in this way; your conscious focus determines what understanding you are interested in, being aware of and understanding it. Most of your life identify, analysing and understanding the meaning of words and relevancy to physical organics. Your understanding however has only been possible by a lot of thought regarding your words and its meaning.

The more complexity you identify with within your consciousness, the more understanding of it you will have. To appreciate why something is simple or easy you first need to stand from a position greater than it is. Interestingly the more complexity you allow yourself to understand because the energy is lighter you can understand more.

The Layers of Understanding run through perceptions of physical matter, form of matter, structure of matter, resonance of matter, movement of matter. To perceive relevancies in physical objects or conversations (people), perceive it as it is physically. This is the What of Understanding, a lot of knowledge regarding what things are in the world.

To perceive relevancies to you about physical objects, perceive in forms, the build of the physical. The how (the meaning) it is, like properties of its physical form. Physical perception relates to physical meaning or understanding. Thoughts regarding it relate to its thoughts of it becoming it. Put yourself mentally as that object or person and relate your thoughts about you but relate from the other (object or person).

To understand the physical or words, you need to focus your attention or consciousness to everything physical or solid, words or physical actions. Within the words exists its form.

To Understanding your Thoughts and how your thoughts perceive this and that, you must focus on just your thoughts, live a life of thoughts. Go about observing everything you know (memories), everything you are doing, aware of and establish a focus of thoughts. Firstly identify you have thoughts and your thoughts do this and do that, watch them form into this and form into that.

Emotion relates to structure of physical or forms. Less and less emphasis is on the density of matter.

Physical is Detail, or words representing energy

Thoughts are Forms or build of energy

Emotions are Structures or shapes of energy

Senses are Resonances of energy

Densities of Perception

Words

All through your life you have been driving a focus of perceiving through words, allow words to give you understanding, your physical movements of being human. Because the conscious focus is at a layer of physical perception, you perceive physically in a linear manner. Your consciousness associates and relates everything in its physical perception. Your sub-conscious however has had to deliver that sub-conscious perception to your consciousness perception. Did not even realise at first perception has layers to it or that could perceive in different ways. Through words and understanding, meaning through words gives a condensed understanding, denser than say your thoughts.

Thoughts

Perceiving through thoughts gives you a greater understanding than when using words. The reason for this is that it takes less energy to deliver the density of thoughts than to deliver words. Your understanding then can increase more so than your understanding of words. Why you think a lot, and get a lot of stress and headaches because you keep intensifying what you choose to understand as words. The less you try to produce mentally as words or physical actions, the less pressure on your mind. Going on holiday you do exactly that, release the pressures by not thinking of the physical work you do. You slowly release pressure over days of the holiday to relax by changing your environment causing you to appreciate lighter physical surroundings than to drive or deliver more of a physical intensity.

Emotions

Emotions are the same in method to understanding; imagine a reality where emotions used as means of conversation or discussion rather than words or thoughts. You still use your mind but relate everything emotionally rather than thinking of words or objects. You identify with everything emotionally and access knowledge of emotions without forming thoughts or words. Less energy needed to deliver density or layer, the greater the understanding. When you have a deep and meaningful conversation, it is just that you are delivery an emotional meaning to the situation in hand.

Senses

Presence or vibrations of self, the feeling of vibrations, or feeling the energy that runs through you. The likeness is meditating on a permanent basis while walking around or working and everything is serene. Build a reality of that and words or thoughts will not affect you or influence you. Take practice to sustain your resonance to a centred being.

Everything here is about work, you need to work at it to allow yourself to be aware, and change it. It is not for someone else to tell you what to do, it is for you to appreciate knowledge or understanding, respect it. Understand it the way you see relevant consciously and then apply action to change your attitudes or mannerisms. The more you understand about your resonance, those senses you have and not just the common senses, the more you will understand about your emotions, thought forms, and words or physical actions.

The tourney that takes a long time is one that integrates more detail and understanding to the subject or title. Focus of commitment continues by focused intent to deliver quality over speed. Perceptions of how fast or slow something offer to be is based on current perception of the individuals perception. Create the world you see by perceiving it, as is then also acting or conversing in a manner to suit the new desired reality.

Perception is what you currently understand about something it is the position of intent towards understanding something and it is just an energy module, part of your whole being. This has been a driving force for thousands of years defining a little perception of what is currently now understood. You have ability to understand far more than you can currently comprehend. Knowing how to use your perception gives you an added benefit to using it wisely. Changing from a perception of knowing a little to knowing a lot more is an act of faith from yourself to develop your soul and evolve your being. The more you understand the easier life becomes because you will be aware of and address what is necessary to address that you consciously understand. What you do not understand yet you have no need to worry about because of knowing that when the moment is due to address you will understand what is necessary to do.

To be able to Perceive you first must have observed something, before you were able to observe you must have been aware before you become aware something had to be there to be aware. Let yourself be present with everything in every way and the result will be awareness of all that exists. The method is the same in any layer of existence whereby you become aware then you observe it then you perceive it your way and believe it, which defines your alignment with your perception of reality. Everything is just energy. Your consciousness is just energy.

We are the construct of energy into this incredible system of being human, by our own making. Associate all your memories in new ways, everything you can think of, Perceive in another way of perception and watch your understanding of it change. The benefit here is you get to choose the association of what perception best suits you, or your memory.

Energies Layers and Trends

Did you know that there are layers to your understanding for perceiving or comprehending? There is also different ways or types to comprehend, different ways to perceive and believe. If you choose not to believe, you can still perceive if you choose not to perceive you can still observe if you choose not to observe you can still be aware.

A theory on dimensional energy, and find it quite interesting. See how it relates to consciousness's and understanding things about you. Call it layers if you like rather than dimensions.

Your consciousness is not linear, it is dimensional so you have to start perceiving and comprehending what you know and see and do in a dimensional manner. Not just accepting the linear point-to-point relevance but the dimensional relevance brings in the resonance, vibrations of words, the forms of thoughts associated with the conversation, the emotions, or density pronouncing the words, the resonance of the essence of what is present from someone to another. The more depth or broadness you perceive the more you will grow that understanding in the little things you perceive and duly grow that depth and broadness for greater insights to the greater things in life. You define your understanding this way, a little or a lot.

Awareness

Awareness is point of observation before making a rule or notion that it is this or that. Without awareness, you have nothing to observe. Awareness is a key aspect to understanding; different people have different scopes or ranges of awareness. You can change and increase your awareness by intending it to be greater than it currently is. Taking an apple as example, do not just be aware that it is an apple, grow your awareness by intending to see more depth to the apple, how it becomes an apple, how it is presently shaped, how it tastes, the types of tastes, how it smells. Do this to everything and increase to universal awareness by being aware of other people and their depths. The town you live in and its depths or content, and all its grandeur. By intending to be aware, you will notice things relevant by observing them and giving growth to your understanding in the same way.

Be aware of its physical properties, how it looks, how it is shaped. Be aware of its form of physical properties, its functions, its methods of becoming apple, its needs, and its trends of life. Be aware of its structure of its forms, and physical properties, the shape, the structure of its taste, its design. Be aware of its resonance, the colours, and the vibrancy of the apple. You define your awareness by choosing to be aware of it; it can only show you its own self. The more you intent to be aware the more your awareness will grow about anything that you are aware of, but you need to do it with everything you can be aware.

Observation

Many different areas to observe from, you are aware of, vision, sense, smell, sounds, taste, touch and then duly deeper visions, deeper sense, deeper smells, deeper sounds, deeper tastes. A good intent is what lies behind what you are observing.

As above from awareness you use your current understanding of forms, structures (physical and organic), its resonance and increase or deepen or broaden that observation to observe more, read books, internet articles regarding it and take your understanding about it from your observations.

The process the same as before: Observe its physical properties, how it looks, how it is shaped. Observe its form of physical properties, its functions, its methods of becoming (an apple), its needs, and its trends of life. Observe its structure of its forms, and physical properties, the shape, the structure of its taste, its design. Observe its resonance, the colours, and the vibrancy of the apple. You define your observation by choosing to observe more of it; it can only show you its own self, how it is. The more you observe the more your observation will grow about anything that you observe, but you need to do it with everything you can observe.

Perception

Defining the relevancy to your consciousness, consciously associating what is important to your understanding. Perception and comprehension are your conscious way of saying this is relevant to life right now; want to know about this object in life. How much and how little you choose to become aware of or observe increases your understanding to perceive. You can perceive a little or a lot.

When you perceive take into account all that you can observe, its forms, physical properties, colours, structure, existence (how it came to be), the vibrancy, the taste. The more you perceive the more your perception will grow about anything that you perceive, but you need to do it with everything you can perceive.

Belief

Belief follows your perception, this is the bit where you can understand what someone has said to you, but your perception has more of an understanding or has a broader understanding that can add to it. Usually both parties get to an understanding consciously so that sub-consciously they both can understand more about the subject or object. Continuing to increase your awareness, observation, and perception you will find you will have a need to have less and less conversations about things, because you will already know the understanding of what is on discussion.

Belief is what defines your position of consciousness, whereas forms maybe important to you of an object or subject whereas the other party the physical structure is important, together you can converse so that the two positions can be understood from either of you.

Overview

All of above are relevant morning, noon, night you do this day in and day out and have been all your life so changing the trends consciously of how you observe or perceive are going to take time. To get to your current understanding you have disregarded a lot information about things or objects by saying I don't what to know, I'm not interested in that, so sub-consciously you hold this understanding greater than your conscious understanding because you're basically saying my consciousness does not want to know. Sub-consciously you are obtaining all this insight about all things.

Throughout your life, you have been restricting the way you understand by decreasing your conscious awareness, observation, perception, and belief, so now you have a limited understanding of everything you can know. Whole of reality is like this presently. Some people are working on improving that conscious understanding others are still decreasing that conscious understanding, but sub-consciously everyone is taking note and building trends or routines that allow them to continue doing it the way they believe and relate too physically. Important to note that, every person has chosen this, but after a few years of doing it you leave more and more understanding to your sub-conscious. Reality drives you to do this by focusing attention to what is deemed relevant for you right now, rather than what is relevant for you to relate to right now.

Energies Densities and Mass

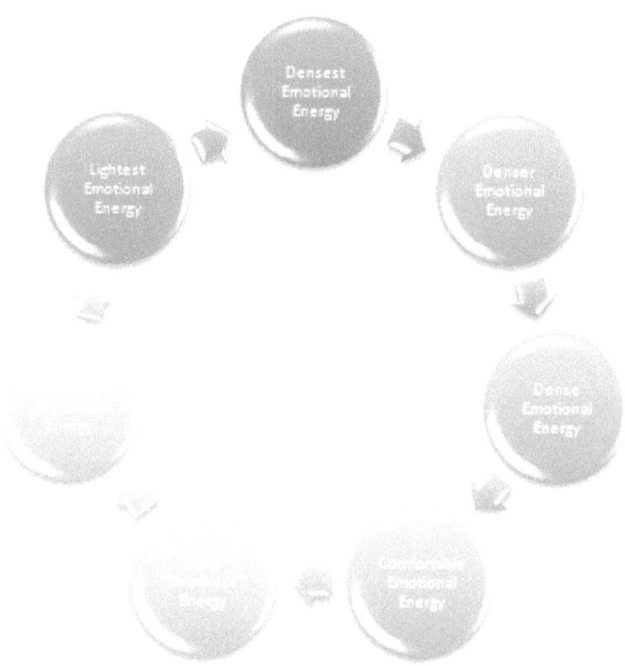

Understanding Emotional Densities

There are others, understanding physical, understanding thought forms, understanding vibrations, resonance, and understanding movement of energy with you. Picked emotions, as many people will be working through that degree of themselves to heal or understand more.

Comfortable Emotional Energy

This is your centred and balanced self, where you have no reason to cry or shout and no reason to laugh and be ecstatically happy. It is the middle or tower of the weighing scales where you can go this way lighter or that way heavier with your emotions.

Any emotion can be changed this way or that, when you are in that moment of an emotion you can change it this way or that way. The comfortable aspect is referring to the centred self. Feel that emotion as lighter than if you were intensely pushing or driving yourself to get something and heavier than if, you are in a meditation or relaxed state. On practicing each day, you will notice these differences as you go about what you do.

Dense, Denser, Densest

These elements are about when you drive or strive for something you continuously put more and more energy or pressure to it so you are building denser energy to obtain it, which is why you get this release or feel good factor when obtained because you release that pressure back to your comfortable self. This does mean though that you are setting trends to apply that pressure for things you want. Each time you do add more pressure you will adjust to, so the comfortable state goes with you. Overtime of doing just that repeatedly your focus being on what you wanted, not focusing on your comfortable state has moved along denser and denser.

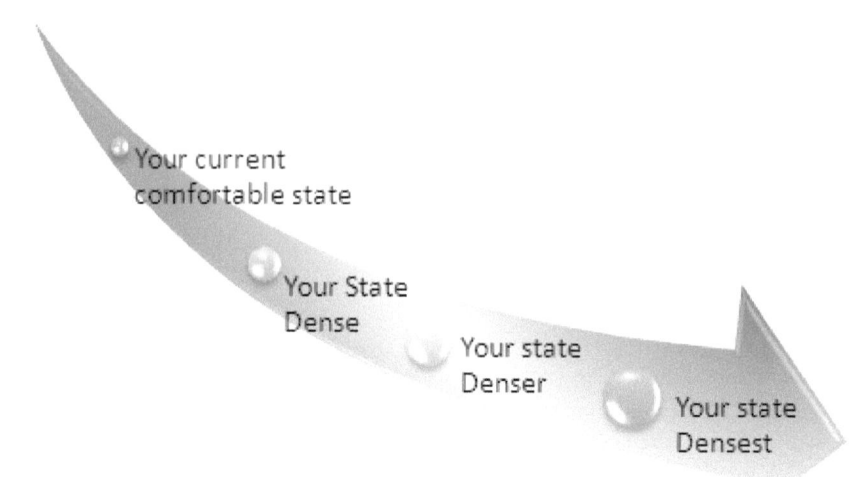

Your energy states getting denser as you drive or intensify your needs or desires, creating more pressures on you. Gets what you need faster, but with less understanding.

Light, Lighter, Lightest

These elements are about the letting go of things, the application of less pressure for your need or desire. The lighter you perceive things, the lighter you resonate as a being. You keep lightening the perception of things, objects or conversations, mannerisms and attitudes you will lessen the pressure to yourself and carry your comfort state into a lighter resonance, less friction. Your understanding will increase as your consciousness shifts with it so that your perception that lightens overtime will perceive more in a moment as less density is sustain in your perception.

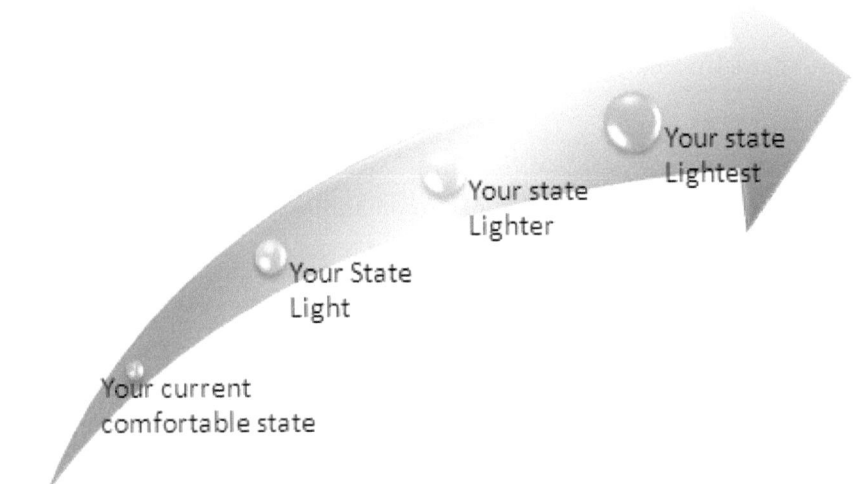

Your energy states getting light as you drive less or intensify less your needs or desires, creating less pressures on you. Gets what you need slower but with greater understanding.

Sadness (Anger or Hate)

We all have it, we all want less of it, and we all can.

Understanding How To: "Identify, Maintain and Decrease"

Identifying your Sadness

Important to note, when you are Sad, know that you are Sad.

Figure 1.0 (Helping to Understanding your Sad).

Picture a moment when you are Sad. Take away the picture and feel the emotions you have knowing that you are Sad. The image is not what makes you Sad your choice of associating the emotion to the image or event that occurred. The feeling can be associated to anything. Practice with various pictures or memories and see or feel the emotion of Sadness. You define what 'Sadness' is to you. Different people associate different degrees or densities of Sadness. The person that is smiling but sad, the demoralizing person holding back tears but still Sad. Think of a genuine sadness streaming from within expressing itself outwardly through a tear to share.

The reason Sadness does not last is not that it goes away; we associate more or other associations to things at a greater degree than of Sadness. The secret is with Sadness is to identify with that inner emotion that you feel Sad enough then associate that with everything you do, are doing and going to do.

The birth of a newborn child brings emotional high to most people, leaving Sadness in the distance. The wedding day full of love and laughter again ascends your normal sad emotion to a greater Happiness. Key to development is to work at being Happier, identify with objects or conversations as sad ones. Over the years, we associate so many emotions to so many things or types of conversations or mannerisms of people; we keep allowing ourselves to change our sad mode to a greater sad mode or de-moralized, depressed state.

Figure 1.1 (Trends of Being Sad)

Gaining weight or force, the more associations we make from a sad emotional state the more force or energy we associate to a sad emotional state. The more we continue to do it, the easier it becomes and less of a task to keep thinking about associating a sad emotional state to everything. Sub-consciously you write routines and trends so that your choices are then automatic or instinctive.

Maintaining your Sadness

Once you have a hold on your Sadness you can play with it. Start by picking things you do that you do not particularly have an emotional feeling towards and practice associating your sad emotional state to it, watch it change, or how you change towards it. This is about reading your emotions and once you get a hold of them you will want to know more about how your emotions affect your thoughts, words, physical actions.

The management is all within your control as designed or associated consciously, so the more you associate with your sad emotional state the more you will understand about things that make you sad. Instead of just the few sad moments in your life, you will soon have hundreds then thousands until it will be difficult not to be anything else other than sad all of the time. When you are sad, guess what, you just change your sad emotion to a happy emotion and become happy.

Figure 1.2 (Maintaining a New Direction)

This does take practice and not just a few weeks, best way to describe this is as a child I was happy about everything I was doing and slowly to a state where everything I was doing made me sad or depressed. 20 years later, it took that long, slowly but surely associated more and more sadness to things and eventually, there was hardly any happiness to notice at all. The practice and maintenance is about reversing that and it is a lot quicker than 20 years. Within weeks and months you will practice, notice and change the way you want to associate your sadness to things. The only person you have to worry about is you doing it.

Density and Pressure, is about force, if you push hard at associating emotions to something they are denser or harsher, depending on how much pressure you are putting on your action of applying or associating happy emotional state to something. The trick is to do it, meaning to apply or associate your happy emotional state to something but apply it or associate it lightly. This in turn gathers weight or force by adding too each time you apply or associate you are happy to something. Greater happiness exists and you can have it. Just apply and associate lightly so the pressure is not harsh or denser than your current sadness emotional state.

Decreasing your Sadness

When applying or associating your sad emotional state to objects, conversations, mannerisms, attitudes, events the key to decreasing is to apply or associate slightly less pressure than before. This needs your own identification of how sad you are currently and then associating a happier emotional state. Difficult to describe but imagine on week 1 you have a sad emotional state, you are comfortable, not overly sad, and not happy. Your sad emotional state would then be something below comfortable. You apply or associate your happy emotional state to various events, occurrences, and people. During the course a few weeks, comfortable state becomes less than your week 1 sad emotional state. You are happier than you were at week 1.

<u>Figure 2.0 (Difficult Influences)</u>

Decreasing your sad emotional state means that you now need a new happy emotional state, one that is happier than the comfortable sad state you have currently. This you keep doing so that each time you feel sad you keep identifying and apply or associating a higher or lighter happier emotional state. Applying or associating a state of happiness too high will lead you to come back to your comfortable state, which you will feel sad because of decreasing you're happy emotional state to you're comfortable state.

Practicing and identifying your current emotional state gives you the ability to keep increasing your happiness and sustaining it.

Figure's and Diagrams

Figure 1.0 (Helping to Understanding your Sadness)

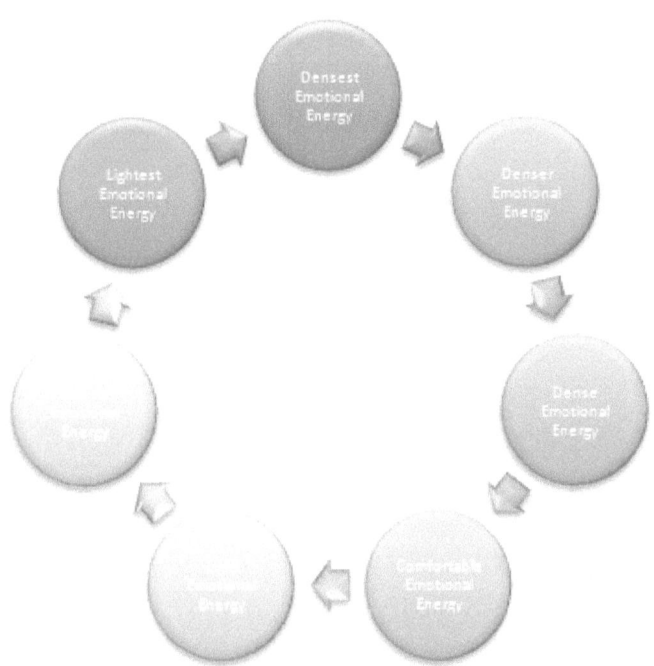

Dense/Denser/Densest: Refers to extent of emotional pressure. The harshest emotions mean the densest or most pressure.

Light/Lighter/Lightest: Refers to the least extent of emotional pressure, or release of pressure. The lightest emotions mean the lightest more angelic or least pressure.

Comfortable: Refers to the balance of your emotions. This is where you feel most comfortable at present. Then you can increase or decrease pressure or more/less energy you put into something.

Example 1: Think of how you say Hello when in a good mood and then how you say Hello in a bad mood. The difference is the range of pressure's you apply. The denser sounding, low, Hello in a bad mood is denser than the High sounding Hello in a good mood. You can change the words but the pressures remain the same. You are comfortable in the middle.

Example 2: Think of how you say Hello to a friend, Happy, open, kind and how you say Hello to a stranger, different. You are not as open or as friendly until you know them. Differences are the pressure you apply. You still do it or say it, but you apply a gentler, harmonic, approach to friends than you do strangers. Try a friendly Hello to a stranger.

Back to <u>Identifying your Sadness</u> (Page 48)

Figure 1.1 (Trends of Being Sad)

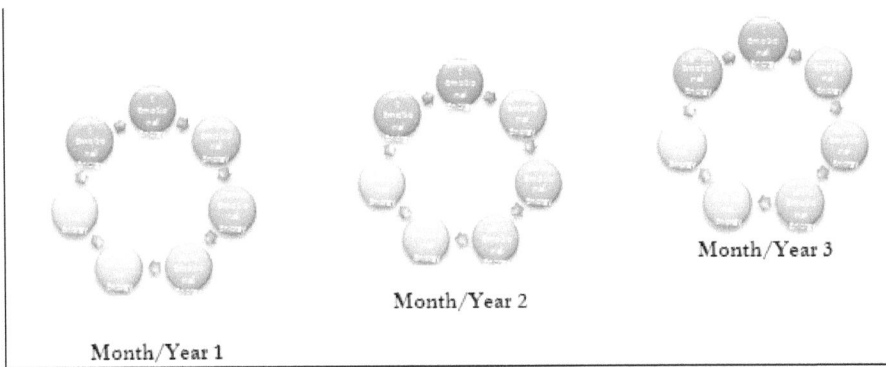

Month/Year 1: The more we apply pressure or intensity to something we say, or something do we increase that pressure overtime. The more energy each time we use to intensify desire or need the more pressure we apply. Meaning: You are still comfortably sad but could be comfortably happier.

Month/Year 2: Is the same but slightly denser than before. These are very fine adjustments. Based on what we do in a moment and keep doing the same way we set trends of how we want to do it. This then creates motions of trends of how we want to do it so we create more pressure and more sadness.

Month/Year 3: Before we have recognized we created this, we are more stressed and denser than we remember. We do not even recognise how we did it.

Back to <u>Maintaining your Sadness</u> (Page 49)

Figure 1.2 (Maintaining a New Direction)

Month/Year 1: Applying less pressure or intensity to what we do or say. Keep associating a lighter, kindly, gentler approach to what you do and less pressure will apply to it.

Month/Year 2: Each time you practice the gentler, friendlier approach keep the momentum going. Associate with everything you are thinking or feeling about this and that. When you become comfortable and happier, keep going, and doing the same, applying a lighter, gentler approach to it.

Month/Year 3: Before you know it, you will see changes and adjustment towards your feelings that are of a happier position than before. Keep going. You will notice changes frequently as long as you are aware and observe what you are doing. The saying "Less is more" is appropriate for this. You still do everything you need to daily just with a little different approach with knowledge of why you are doing it.

The happiest feeling you can feel can be the comfortable, average, or normal feeling.

Back to Maintaining your Sadness (Page 49)

Figure 2.0 (Difficult Influences)

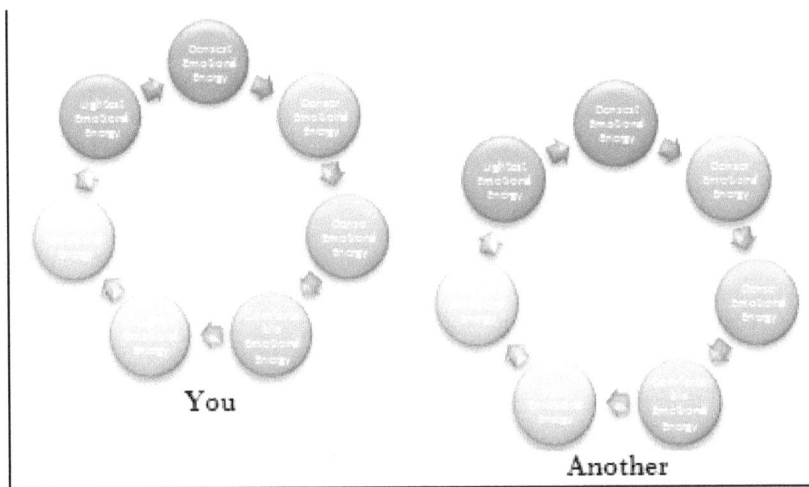

                      You   Another

     Talking with someone or working with someone generates an emotional connection. This connection influences you and your sadness. A depressed person will influence denser emotions (sadness) whereas a light-hearted person influences a lighter emotion (happiness). No blame is associated unless you think it, not being anyone's fault it is just his or her understanding of him or her. The important factor is to know that you are feeling denser or lighter. Lighter is good to understand how you can increase your happiness towards what you are both doing, a transaction, or job. Whereas to other, denser is to sustain or maintain sadness or what is comfortable to you which in turn is influencing the other.

     Strict responsibility (free will) falls to the individual that they do what they want to do, whether they see it or not, whether you like it or not. Just change and adjust your emotional state for you.

     Back to <u>Decreasing your Sadness</u> (Page 50)

Practice Tasks

Task 1 - *Identifying*

Identifying your sadness on a regular basis builds a better understanding towards how it is, when it changes and gives you ability or opportunity to change it whenever necessary. Try not to pressurise yourself doing it but take a regular look inside to see sad feeling or not.

Task 2 - *Maintaining*

Maintaining your sadness follows identification. Identify then maintain. Depending how you feel adjust accordingly, not too much at one time but just enough so you feel a change in your mood.

Task 3 - *Decreasing*

Decreasing your sadness follows maintaining it. Once you adjust your mood and feel comfortable again, increase your happiness, to feel happier. Perceive it and believe it then the feeling will increase.

Task 4 - *Cycle*

Repeat the cycle of Tasks 1-3 repeatedly but do not force them. Keep a regular eye or thought on them in order.

Task 5 - *Reread*

Reread this document for first few weeks then few months. This is to keep an understanding to why you doing this so that your intent of decreasing sadness is part of the whole process. Key words like Happy, Happiness regularly used within this document to help bestow your desire of happiness.

Task 6 – *Go Slowly*

Go slowly; reason why a gentler approach towards the tasks creates a lighter pressure than rushing or pushing the tasks like a mission. More pressure equals denser outcome (sadness). Less pressure equals lighter outcome (happiness).

Happiness (Love or Peace)

We all have it, we all want more of it, and we all can.

Understanding How To: "Identify, Maintain and Increase"

Identifying your Happiness

Important to note, when you are Happy, know that you are Happy.

Figure 1.0 (Helping to Understanding your Happy).

Picture a moment when you are Happy. Take away the picture and feel the feelings you have knowing that you are Happy. The image is not what makes you Happy your choice of associating the feeling to the image or event that occurred. The feeling can be associated to anything. Practice with various pictures or memories and see or feel the emotion of Happiness. You define what 'Happiness' is to you. Different people associate different degrees or densities of Happiness. The overbearing person that is ecstatically happy, the demoralized person forcing a smile but still Happy. Think of a genuine happy smile streaming from within expressing itself outwardly through a smile to share.

The reason Happiness does not last is not that it goes away; we associate more or other associations to things at a lesser degree of Happiness. The secret is with Happiness is to identify with that inner emotion that you feel Happy enough then associate that with everything you do, are doing and going to do.

The birth of a newborn child brings emotional high to most people. The wedding day full of love and laughter again ascends your normal happy emotion to a greater Happiness. Key to development is to work at being Happy, identify with objects or conversations as happy ones. Over the years, we associate so many emotions to so many things or types of conversations or mannerisms of people, we keep allowing ourselves to change our happy mode to a not so happy mode or de-moralized, depressed state.

Figure 1.1 (Trends of Being Happy)

Gaining weight or force, the more associations we make from a happy emotional state the more force or energy we associate to it, happy emotional state.

The more we continue to do it, the easier it becomes and less of a task to keep thinking about associating happy emotional state to everything. Sub-consciously you write routines and trends so that your choices are then automatic or instinctive.

Maintaining your Happiness

Once you have a hold on your Happiness you can play with it. Start by picking things you do that you do not particularly have an emotional feeling towards and practice associating your happy emotional state to it, watch it change, or how you change towards it. This is about reading your emotions and once you get a hold of them you will want to know more about how your emotions affect your thoughts, words, physical actions.

The management is all within your control as designed or associated consciously, so the more you associate with your happy emotional state the more you will understand about things that make you happy. Instead of just the few happy moments in your life, you will soon have hundreds then thousands until it will be difficult not to be anything else other than happy all of the time. When you are not happy, guess what, you just change and become happy.

Figure 1.2 (Maintaining a New Direction)

This does take practice and not just a few weeks, best way to describe it is as a child I was happy about everything I was then doing and slowly got to a state where everything was sad or depressed. 20 years later, it took that long, slowly but surely associated less and less happiness to things and eventually, there was hardly any happiness to notice at all. The practice and maintenance is about reversing that and it is a lot quicker than 20 years. Within weeks and months you will practice, notice and change the way you want to associate your happiness to things. The only person you have to worry about is you doing it.

Density and Pressure, is about force, if you push hard at associating emotions to something they are denser or harsher, depending on how much pressure you are putting on your action of applying or associating happy emotional state to something. The trick is to do it, meaning to apply or associate your happy emotional state to something but apply it or associate it lightly. This in turn gathers weight or force by adding too each time you apply or associate your happy emotional state to something. Greater happiness exists and you can have it. Just apply and associate lightly so the pressure is not harsh or denser than your current happy emotional state.

Increasing your Happiness

When applying or associating your happy emotional state to objects, conversations, mannerisms, attitudes, events the key to increasing is to apply or associate slightly less pressure than before. This needs your own identification of how happy you are currently and then associating a happier emotional state. Difficult to describe but image on week 1 you have a happy emotional state, you are comfortable, not overly happy, and not sad. Your happy emotional state would then be something above comfortable. You apply or associate your happy emotional state to various events, occurrences, and people. During the course a few weeks, the comfortable state becomes your week 1 happy emotional state. You are happier than you were at week 1.

Figure 2.0 (Difficult Influences)

Increasing your happy emotional state means that you now need a new happy emotional state, one that is happier than the comfortable state you have currently. This you keep doing so that each time you feel not so happy you keep identifying and apply or associating a higher or lighter happier emotional state. Applying or associating a state of happiness too high will lead you to come back to your comfortable state, which you will feel sad because of decreasing you're happy emotional state to you're comfortable state.

Practicing and identifying your current emotional state gives you the ability to keep increasing your happiness and sustaining it.

Figure's and Diagrams

Figure 1.0 (Helping to Understanding your Happy)

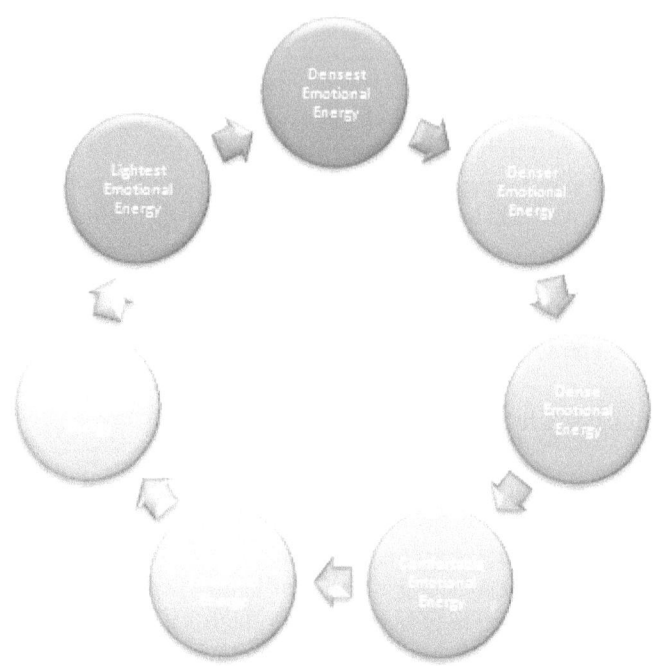

Dense/Denser/Densest: Refers to extent of emotional pressure. The harshest emotions mean the densest or most pressure.

Light/Lighter/Lightest: Refers to the least extent of emotional pressure, or release of pressure. The lightest emotions mean the lightest more angelic or least pressure.

Comfortable: Refers to the balance of your emotions. This is where you feel most comfortable at present. Then you can increase or decrease pressure or more/less energy you put into something.

Example 1: Think of how you say Hello when in a good mood and then how you say Hello in a bad mood. The difference is the range of pressure's you apply. The denser sounding, low, Hello in a bad mood is denser than the High sounding Hello in a good mood. You can change the words but the pressures remain the same. You are comfortable in the middle.

Example 2: Think of how you say Hello to a friend, Happy, open, kind and how you say Hello to a stranger, different. You are not as open or as friendly until you know them. Differences are the pressure you apply. You still do it or say it, but you apply a gentler, harmonic, approach to friends than you do strangers. Try a friendly Hello to a stranger.

Back to Identifying your Happiness (Page 57)

Figure 1.1 (Trends of Being Happy)

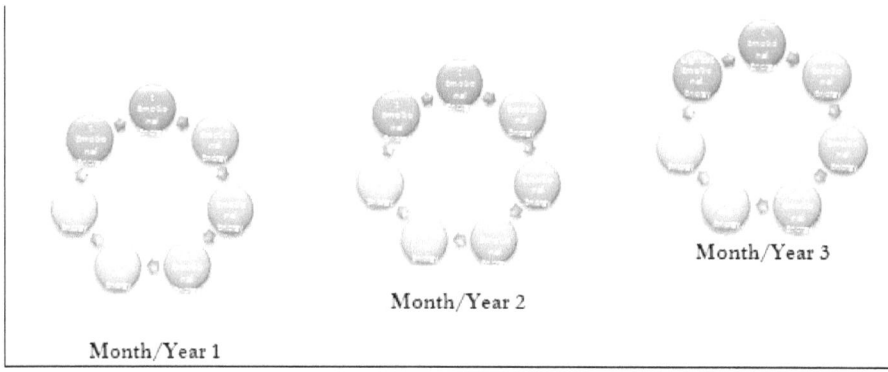

      Month/Year 1: The more we apply pressure or intensity to something we say, or something do we increase that pressure overtime. The more energy each time we use to intensify desire or need the more pressure we apply. Meaning: You are still comfortably happy but could be comfortably happier.

      Month/Year 2: Is the same but slightly denser than before. These are very fine adjustments. Based on what we do in a moment and keep doing the same way we set trends of how we want to do it. This then creates motions of trends of how we want to do it so we create more pressure and more stress.

      Month/Year 3: Before we have recognized we created this, we are more stressed and denser than we remember. We do not even recognise how we did it.

Back to <u>Maintaining your Happiness</u> (Page 58)

Figure 1.2 (Maintaining a New Direction)

Month/Year 1: Applying less pressure or intensity to what we do or say. Keep associating a lighter, kindly, gentler approach to what you do and less pressure will apply to it.

Month/Year 2: Each time you practice the gentler, friendlier approach keep the momentum going. Associate with everything you are thinking or feeling about this and that. When you become comfortable and happier, keep going, and doing the same, applying a lighter, gentler approach to it.

Month/Year 3: Before you know it, you will see changes and adjustment towards your feelings that are of a happier position than before. Keep going. You will notice changes frequently as long as you are aware and observe what you are doing. The saying "Less is more" is appropriate for this. You still do everything you need to daily just with a little different approach with knowledge of why you are doing it.

The happiest feeling you can feel can be the comfortable, average, or normal feeling.

Back to Maintaining your Happiness (Page 58)

Figure 2.0 (Difficult Influences)

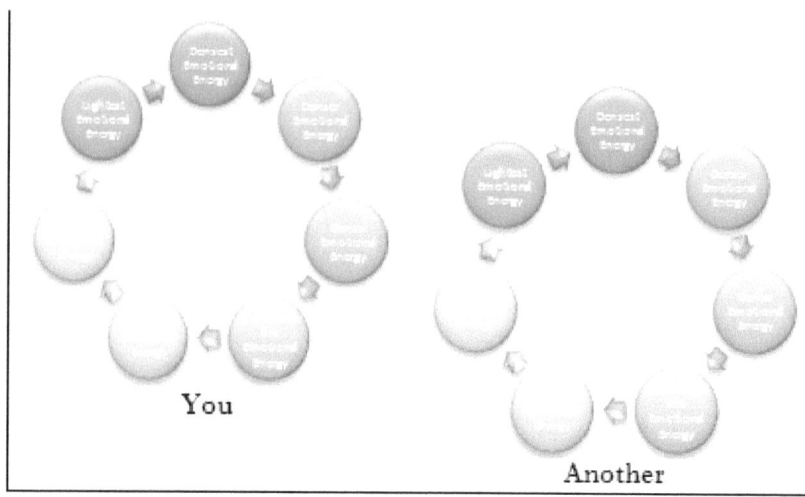

Talking with someone or working with someone generates an emotional connection. This connection influences you and your happiness. A depressed person will influence denser emotions whereas a light-hearted person influences a lighter emotion. No blame is associated unless you think it, not being anyone's fault it is just his or her understanding of him or her. The important factor is to know that you are feeling denser or lighter. Lighter is good to understand how you can increase your happiness towards what you are both doing, a transaction, or job. Whereas to other, denser is to sustain or maintain what is comfortable to you which in turn is influencing the other.

Strict responsibility (free will) falls to the individual that they do what they want to do, whether they see it or not, whether you like it or not. Just change and adjust your emotion state.

Back to Increasing your Happiness (Page 59)

Practice Tasks

Task 1 - Identifying

Identifying your happiness on a regular basis builds a better understanding towards how it is, when it changes and gives you ability or opportunity to change it whenever necessary. Try not to pressurise yourself doing it but take a regular look inside to see happy feeling or not.

Task 2 - Maintaining

Maintaining your happiness follows identification. Identify then maintain. Depending how you feel adjust accordingly, not too much at one time but just enough so you feel a change in your mood.

Task 3 - Increasing

Increasing your happiness follows maintaining it. Once you adjust your mood and feel comfortable again, increase your happiness, to feel happier. Perceive it and believe it then the feeling will increase.

Task 4 - Cycle

Repeat the cycle of Tasks 1-3 repeatedly but do not force them. Keep a regular eye or thought on them in order.

Task 5 - Reread

Reread this document for first few weeks then few months. This is to keep an understanding to why you doing this so that your intent of happiness is part of the whole process. Key words like Happy, Happiness regularly used within this document to help bestow your desire of happiness.

Task 6 – Go Slowly

Go slowly; reason why a gentler approach towards the tasks creates a lighter pressure than rushing or pushing the tasks like a mission. More pressure equals denser outcome. Less pressure equals lighter outcome.

Relating Realities

We currently as human beings have a nice linear overview of everything in the universe; use dynamically on a daily basis inwardly identifying the energies with you. Everyday will be an adventure, every situation a learning curve, every moment a feeling of however you want it to be. The scope of this is enormous in its potential, not just understand the basics but some of the most advance technology the universe has on offer to assist and sustain humanity. The intent of this book is to assist with understanding and awareness by self-example and self-understanding. It is about doing what you normally do with greater depth and understanding; and will make changes that suit your needs and others for the better.

Everything is about making slight changes regarding how, now, then the rest will be your trends and routines that apply to your daily life. No other beings can assist in auctioning this as we created it as human beings. Whether you are an architect or a cleaner, a sales person to a leader the same applies to your manner and attitudes of delivering lighter approaches to what is normal routines.

Each time you relate to something or someone change the way you perceive it and you will start gaining a greater understanding that you currently have. When perceiving allow room for more complexities to be shown about something and do not restrict yourself by stating a way or a thought about how you want it. Understanding it or yourself is different to you wanting to understand it this way or that way.

Life of Insights

October 2004 – October 2006 an incredible journey occurred consciously to understand the energy and systems within the sub-conscious. Herein are some of those early insights along the way.

The book is about deep insight and broader insight from within the depth of the self. How elements or aspects of yourself, words, thoughts, feelings, senses are influencing your awareness, perception, belief to comprehend life consciously in a centred, balanced, practical manner as you go about doing what you do without restrictions of what is known or unknown, orthodox or unorthodox, perceived or not, comprehended or not. Interpretation of universal energies, identify or cross-reference external aspects.

Knowledge, wisdom, and balance are key focuses while going about this journey or transmutation of the self. Understanding that we are a lot greater than we are and have capacity to create anything we desire in line with all else, inclusive of managing the parts within to sustain a greater being. Potential is endless, this book is a start of representing the self's growth into various realities perceivable from the self.

The journey for this book has taken years of digressive and journalistic mannerism (approaching neutrally) into the known and unknown aspects of self to see what works towards the goal, as in the greater self overcoming emotions, senses, thoughts, physical mannerisms and ascending each part to grow the essence or resonance of the soul.

Interestingly structures, designs, mechanics, modules and routes or streams of how the energy fills within and produces all of the aspects of the whole self are presented in a realistic approach herein to represent an attitude towards working with various inner dimensions we currently choose not to be aware of. These are interestingly also represented externally as a means of working environments or structures in today's society or culture. Whether it is a business structure, technological design, engineering practice, and mechanics it relates inwardly.

Explaining the universe from the self in one book is not possible due to restriction of conscious capacity so I've had to brief on the overview of knowledge areas or snapshots to represent deep insights that are represented herein, each of which could plausibly be a book by digressing the detail, each category or content that is. When not reading this book notice your surroundings and inner aspects of your life and how they relate or cross-reference with it.

Enjoy, have fun seeing more of what you do.

The Day is Today

The Day is today. Tomorrow is yet to come. Yesterday has gone. Now is so long.

Presented by the moment with energy of past, present and future we touch on reality, are we here, Yes we are, No we are not. Who cares what it is, to see, to be, we will do what it is within us we feel, instinctively.

We create this way to see what it is each day to be this way in this place to feel in a motion to do, to act on the past to free us from our own mask.

Drive and passion create a dream, driven by many to the foreseen. Me, Myself, and I can always be what it is in mastery of thee.

The need is driven to passionately be as pure as the eye can see, love is blind because it will not be bullied or pushed or pulled or rushed…..it like us drives itself to become bigger, better, purer than before.

See the world with new eyes this day in pubs, clubs, restaurants, cinemas, playgrounds, parks, forests, home, gardens and see how the energy evolves all of the aspects of you.

We feel and guide others, to be, as we deem it necessary and ourselves. We find sad friends for moments of sadness, happy friends for moments of happiness and partners for sharing all moments. The people or properties change as more knowledge gained or more healing needed. See you without time or restrictions, without the need or the wants and respect all others for their requirements and pains. Issues overcome and ascension begun, the earth is writing a book, look and read to see you are a part of its seed. If you could see the energy running within all and understand, why it is to be, all other moralities or concerns will be clear and duly freed. Caught up in the system, this comes to me, frustration and anxiety to release will set a property free.

The properties of what is that we see, emblematic of what it is that needs to be. Form, it shows us all the need to see visually as the stunning blonde walks by and says hi to me. A large woman has interest. The gay or lesbian who needs to be expressively, not frightened to see their type of interests.

One Aim, One Goal

One aim, one goal, one flag, one hole is the easy approach to know. We sit in remembrance of the highs and lows respecting our boundaries, as we know, mastering our properties to show the knowledge, and understanding we know.

From the properties of a computer to a car to a tree to an animal, as a person lives and shines, the world climbs to show how proud the parts of wisdom and creation the elements are.

Knowing what you know and knowing what you need to know and what you do not need know. Doing what you need to do, worrying about what is done, worrying about what needs to be. Through happiness and sadness, pushing through the issue's of the day. Controlling people and healing others. The kind will always focus on kind, the hurtful will focus on hurting, and the angry will focus on anger. The truth will be the balance, the generous complain about the greedy, the people with money give none away, the people without give all they can this day.

Slowly the wheel and ribbons seem to turn presenting a difference in energy time you give, a flavour of the generous heart welcomes, hello is always hello. Goodbye is always goodbye. Come to see these elements within to learn the mirror of what presented to see. Test thyself into understanding, use knowledge, compassion, and understanding to help to achieve all aspects to attain the highest good for all human kind. Being Selfish, Selfhood, Selfless. 1-2-3 it is easy. Morality is a restriction whereas the feeling of immoral is a good feeling. Feel the law if you hurt someone expect to be hurt in the same or another form. If you borrow money, make sure you pay back the amount of generosity in the same or other form, likewise in reverse but do not expect the same back.

Except what it is when it is, planning will manifest the form from the feel within the self to the creation of the moment. The worse moment in your life they will sing and dance all night. The best moment in your life and they sing and dance all night. Masters of all, of none, of some, of many or just one, we are what we are and should be what we should be.

Time is time, without time, there is no rush, with time, and there is a rush. This relates we will time everything when everything is just a moment. A tree will know when to be this way and that does not plan it, does not time it, it is just what it needs to be to renew, refresh, replenish and regenerate or create. "To be or not to be", the answer or the Question?

Through the child that knows, what we know and want to know when born to show what it is that could train into the understanding of our physical reality they will live in. They choose to see to heal the things in. From the wisdom of age through physical reality not needed around to live the life of the present day.

Deal with the truth to see what clear power in is. Every day we climb and every day we will shine. Each individual reality will be the presence of the self.

Through my own abuse physical, mental, and emotional we begin to see clearly, what happiness is to us?

Saw a show about a girl who lies a lot, knows that she lies, and is asking for the change to better herself, those around her dominate her. A woman be Military MP to a controlling aunt, the uncle stuck in a pattern of acceptance and honouring the family finds themselves to not be wrong but the girl that is the happiest she has ever been from a fostered, abused reality, she wants to be in this place where she is bullied. We choose our position for ourselves and change those aspects to better our surroundings. Things are what they are for the individual that is, because we individually manifest it as so. The forms are just reality in the physical that are confusing, read the forms correctly by not trying to read into them, keep it simple, it is what it is.

This is everyday life seen from a perspective necessary to do and be who you have always felt you should be. When absorbed and only then can you move forward? The properties need to be so that knowing what to do and how to do it in those situations avoid, adhere to or healed, passed on.

Touching the Surface of your true reality is about the truth behind the form of the moment in the individual that chooses to see and heal.

Through Thick and Thin

Through thick and thin we see delight and sin, the good and the bad do not make us sad, our pattern will create the emotional turmoil or response and all the time it is meant to be as you asked them to see. I honour those that choose and respect that knows what it is to be free to create all that we see.

Stay tuned in with seeing and what is on show. I remember nothing, I know nothing, I see nothing, I feel nothing, yet I see all I need to see, I remember all I need to remember, I know all that I need to know, I feel all that I need to feel. Consciously I create all that holds me up to date.

The answer lies within no answer, the question is within no question. The words are just a form; the writing is also a means to create an energy that is so great. Thick or thin, hard or soft it is there, is it not. I stand in front of a mirror and my sight slightly out of focus to see what is true in me, a reflection it is not, no image of form to see, just nothing in the mirror of me.

Guided as one we see all those traits within others their patterns to love or hate. Books to reveal, emails to carry communicate those forms to love and marry. As I cry in my seat at a coffee shop in the street I feel the strain that comes from pain and yet they will not quit they continue to exist, creating a way to live every day, I honour the compassion for self creation. To better existence in all that exists.

We are what we are

We are what we are in a world of near and far. We see what we see based on the design of thee. We feel what it is in a development stage we seek. To live life to the full feel all and love all makes the prouder and prouder to us all. Through the rough and through the thin, the simple life I long to sing, complicate the complicated to stand where you are. Discuss the possible and stand where you are, ifs, and not's that show things too far.

Develop us all, through the young and the small. Time to listen to what is being said not just hearing what they say. Time to trust in those that fight to achieve and under achieve what they allow to which restricts them.

Through the drive that we seek, the friends that we meet, the search begun to the only one. The one is all in a property of a ball, the same on the inside as well as the out. What is it we see and scream? They show us all day in every way what we need to know about. Colours and clouds we see a loud to show the world what it is.

Earlier today, I saw little flies flying around in my eyes, Bright and white they glow all day preparing me for what has to come and know this way. Enjoy the moment as we see it will pass and to the next adventure at long awaited last.

Formations of Properties

Formations of properties from one to the other create a balance in the whole.

I see all Human kind in properties of adjustment. I move between within and around the properties helping and adjusting. Inside, outside is my work. Leading me to where I need to be.

My visions are vast of global earthly and universal nature. My knowledge comes through all manners of media and communication. I speak little verbally of the conditions knowing the action balances or imbalances the elements.

We know the world as it should be and seek answers to do with thee. The small are vastly bigger as a whole.

My visions, hearing, and speech are now forever different, growing glowing words of wisdom and light. How the earth handles the vast income of adjustment is beyond my current knowledge. Drop a stone in the lake and the whole lake feels the ripple effect. The blue lights I see are warm and comforting.

To be in true balance of you is to be in sole connection with all elements allowing the believable to be unbelievable and the unbelievable to be believable. It is what everyone does one way or another, to choose the chosen to understand whatever they do using the resources, components or knowledge gained this far.

The vast information now coming through is we, ourselves, and us an emblematic metaphor for the existence and workings of all. The growth is leading me to mother earth; how she deals with the elements, touching on universal attributes, build the growth and development of the self for others to follow. I know I need to share this and help in the process of others but I thought I would get to a point whereby I would stay stagnant. It last a month to show me what it was practically and by action and intent then still taking me further, higher and beyond. The belief in knowing what will be for futures to gain and grasp is so enlightening, it has to start soon, yet I find myself going from strength to strength with no long-term reservation to pause or stop.

The books themselves are a means to a development that can balance all aspects of the environment situated within.

The Crystal cluster is amazing with immense earthly knowledge, energy from Camelot that even I have only touched and held the power behind what we combined hold. I regularly send knowledge, information, and love and purity energy to all human kind as a matter of natural course, not consciously creating an image. Depth of knowledge is only as wise as at the time it is used. Only that moment can present true wisdom of the knowledge and wisdom that holds in the moment.

My hands cannot keep up with all that is flowing; the actions can only sum up part of what needs to be. Giving healing miles away, healing for someone without speaking words. All media physical, Mental and Emotional are flowing together. Colours and Numbers are progressing in clarity, signs showing as they never did before, every film has a message, and meaning, every word has a weight carried from within encompassing the elements written or spoken.

The elements that come and strand that are creating into realities understood or not within, begin to create and manifest these words within based on a life style, design or pattern developed to what it is now as I am what I am.

This is just "Touching the Surface". Once reality is absorbed the dimensional reality becomes present, once that then is absorbed the unbelievable becomes believable from once was becomes the realm of the individual that lives it to breathe it and develop it. Through sounds that are not there, through objects seen that do not exist, the smells that have potency in a place they do not belong. I live my life and sing this song.

Changing Patterns

Rainbow Vortex

"Changing Patterns of Material Love for Universal Love"

Tonight, today is the day I started the process of giving up something I love, Emblematic of the materials of life. The changing faces of the inner, loving only real love, gaining no monetary or material valuables.

Since being made redundant money has come enough to get the material things I needed or more so want and materialize. I have reached a turnstile of the self to continue with the material gains or enter a world or worlds of all elements on, within, and around the earth.

Today I gave the intent of the last material aspect, the big one. As soon as the letter entered the letterbox out of my hands on its journey I was welcomed by colours of the rainbow manifesting from my base chakra in a vortex funnel up through my body into the grid above rotating like a tornado (calmer) in at first an anti-clockwise direction slowing down over a period and duly rotating clockwise. Soon after more was coming a beautiful bright white channel coming through from mother earth, now I sit here in a whirlwind of beauty.

Rainbow Vortex

The rainbow vortex is still with me in this morning cool air. The energy is a feel of love, hope, purity in elements of the earth, very calming effect surrounds me now, a feeling of I can do anything. Clockwise rotation is still present swaying from North to South, East to West. Connected to the source of all, the book, the book, the book I am sensing. The book that I write is to show the positive in all as we pass through elements not seen by most of us all, it's to connect with the depth of the self to appreciate what it is we are doing and have done and will do with a knowledgebase we can access at anytime.

Interesting to see all that I see showing a force well beyond me. A pattern emerges that creates a blast of that energy called that we seek through the mask.

I share with all the benefits that stand tall to help and heal the things inside us all. As I master the elements presented to me. I wonder if I can help show everyone to see. Only those that choose to see beyond what they look at will know a true sense of purity.

A dream, a visualisation of what manifests this way is placing me into a realm to gain the pure properties I seek adjusting the bleak to stand tall in it all to show all how neat. Money will come and issues will pass to balance the moment long awaited at last. The money is not for the personal gain it belongs to the elements I service this day. With the consent of all, this wonderful place, this physical reality we continue to create.

I love to start the reality I seek, having resources to hand that will help the growth in its tree. The time will come one day at last and on that moment, we begin a task, a project from the mother that will help show what it be that all humanity wishes to believe. A Earth Station to measure the balance as we see it this day and how we can progress each day. A weather station it is not but a dimensional plain it is as we raise the vibrational level for all our kids.

Crystal Maze

Crystal maze into the heart with white light in directions of North, South, East and west which connects with the Electromagnetic grid.

It all interlinks….

Inside the dome are multiples of the same, it transcends information, knowledge, energy through the system that we gain.

Adjustable, Adaptive to all surroundings like dropping a stone in the pond has ripple effect and we feel\notice very little about the waves until they build. The dome increases and decreases with will and intention to receive, give more to those around you. Affecting the group and adjusting the earth channel within us all.

All media: Telephone, Fax, Email, Letter, Physical, In passing, Dimensional, Thoughtful, Worry, Concern, Happiness, Love, Anger, Hate, Passion, Compassion all means of communication in a dimensional world we live in. The group, groups the priorities being the amalgamation of the clustered energy here within.

Properties of the car: Material gain to hold aspects of the self being, self maintenance, self power, self desires, self feelings, time to call back those properties left in the past now current in other forms. Friends will carry some properties for you; work will carry others, banks, homes even more. You choose to use these properties at your leisure when a need regular or irregular is required to for fill your journey's requests from you.

If the Wind Blows

If the wind blows, the world begins to show what it is we need to know to hold onto what we know to develop the knowledge of how we know it, knowing we just need to be knowledgeable of where we know we should be.

The world has menace and mice to run the problems from thrice, they change the way we are with properties from afar, true to form, set to be in the life they live for thee. They have issues of vast to battle to be at last in the essence the need to be free. We sit here and judge what they aspire instead of see what they have aspired. We push for the best in all others to restrain the need in us to do the work. Forever more we will see their fight with such force and might. They show it in a way that we see this day for their lives they live are un-shadowed by the day. From a moment, they will in ore or thee and back again into reality.

Formulation of Book

Formulation of book, creative ideas based upon experience and knowledge of the physical realm tasked and created firstly before action of form manifested by means of channelled interpretation of the said best current form of understanding the layers within the book. Build from basic, simple words into complex understanding by means of depth translation from words to reality.

The form is paramount whether one book, two books, Volumes, Little Transcripts, Poems, How presented, how Built, How Seen, How Perceived, How Written.

Energy Transference

The person downstairs thought it necessary to knock on my door and state that my T.V. was too noisy and vibrating his ceiling, I kindly advised I would turn the T.V. down and apologised for the Noise.

What actually occurred?

All properties pertaining to this issue positive for him and negative to me transferred. His persona changed while talking while receiving positive energy from me, releasing his negative pent-up energy into me. Caught off guard I was, ready to receive, without protection and not firmly grounded, as I should be. I have now, for days taken on those properties to heal them, understand them, and pass them back over cleansed. He may never know the amount of work taken to heal the properties within him, although continuing his pattern will regenerate them again.

Every moment in my flat in or around encased with the properties the forms were restlessness, fear, anger, kindness, generosity, frustration, and a need for help. Those elements had negativity in the balance whereas thoughts and desires from me were taking upon these properties from within. As I adjust, send healing to and creating a calmer, clearer, more cleansed and loving approach. The adjustments took 2 days as they relate to multiple areas of the self. Through emotions, feelings, words, and minds the differences felt around me. The worry was increased doe to my concern for fellow man. The controlling aspects of his personal pattern were apparent; see that as one he is fighting himself.

The teachings for me were one of openness to receive. Knowing I have to stay open for attack I also have to protect to balance and avoid the situation happening. Grounding and protection were key elements to me. Fly by, now and then will not suffice anymore. Regular maintenance to establish a consistency within is required to maintain balance necessary to fulfil my destiny from me.

The conscious side of me kicks the drive subconsciously to do, maintaining that is a pattern for always as new. The cycle of the day, the moment I'm awaken into a realm of physical reality must be grounded to "Sink to Source" to stand true always as new to thyself as to be thyself to fulfil the true. Protection follows to protect the source from being abused namely myself from having a flu to see the balance to create the new. Difficult it is to start this quiz, need to allow the process to be absolute.

People are what they are

People are what they are, they do what do they do because of what is within you, you create a reality the people in group connection match it, unless they have cause to raise it or reduce it to feel more comfortable. Do not think all evening look at moments, the highs, the lows, the practical, emotional, physical, the bonding, the balancing, the neutral, the excited, the talented. Encompass and see all the elements in all those around and watch who balances whom with what properties they have, that they want, that they master. Start to see the issues behind, the development process, the pattern that exists, all relates to what, and how they are now.

"Searching"

'Searching for something' that is already there, to fact find, to analyze, to deliberate, to calculate all issues of trust. I was abused when young and had a very fast analytical mind. Maths came easy; school reports showed I can do the hard things but struggled with the easy. Reason being I was always looking for more than the simple answer. It is so easy so I would make up equations to confuse the moment when it is just what it is, simple. In the search you will dissolves and absorb all possible equations within your knowledge of understanding and belief before coming to an answer that was already given that you couldn't see, lost in the process of searching for more, other. More information, more searching, more understanding is expanding the knowledge into the realm, different theories, different practices, methodology or procedure all relate to the conscious using what it knows and creating to build and develop doing what it does because it is designed to do it.

Things become clearer with age when they were always clear as a child without the depth of knowledge, wisdom, and "Morality", why cannot I do this, why cannot I see this. Try not trying to see what you see and what you do, where's the harm in being you, if you do not harm anyone in being themselves. Stop searching for the search and start to see what is.

A writer is becoming apparent in me to send those words of wisdom needed by me, trusted is the words we see every day in how they say "Hello" in her way. The feminine properties needed to blast those words of wisdom received at last, the male properties for the strength and conviction carry those properties to the intended. Both amalgamate what actually is so some of herein is missed.

None is forgotten, all is taken in and when the time is right will be seen not so thin. Taking the moment to grasp all that can be will forever last within thee. I send you this will to see inside what is necessary for you to decide in those moments that you need to digress. Carrying this with you in a dimension of trust and purity helps provide the resources needed inside. For all to begin see without sin. For everything, we receive see it as it is and accept it to be, we build everyday and choose to show it this way. Take what you need from this, this way and continue the journey you have built today.

The realms negative and angry manifested by those patterns of past and group come into a request for help and understanding. Through understanding or choosing realms of possibilities you become encompassed into those properties and act as you need to act to be who you need to be in those surroundings and elements within you. Give up, neglect, ignore, hate and allow all that comes back to come to you and then fight it. See with open eyes how it could be and choose it is an easy process to be happy or sad. Buying into what is not within you, when you feel something should not be then you are in essence asking for trouble, sometimes a good option to overcome a bad situation or pattern within you, but the same for the good in you or group.

You choose, no one else, you just do not have all the facts when the choice made or the respect of what achieved by the choices being chosen. Let it ride on the positive and see where it takes you. If anyone wants to take it away, find another way that does not hurt another and what it is you are attracting. Once the elements of people, human kind have started being absorbed, look at what else is attracting you that you are attracting. Earth, Wind, Fire, Air, Tree's, Leaves, Grass, Animals, Plants…etc…it goes on everywhere. Relevance of the astral plain is then becoming an immense importance just to see or accept advice from all elements, all realms, all dimensions, and all entities.

A very beautiful, innocent, young woman came up to me asked "Excuse me, is anyone using this seat" (in a soft, pleasant, worried and kindly voice).

What actually happened?

So beautiful that people can be I sense a frightened, careful woman, worried about offending, wants to please and help everyone she meets. A lot of Love, Compassion, understanding, awareness, togetherness, "wouldn't hurt a fly" form, looks to go with it as well. Group energy putting into balance what has occurred in the last few days. Thank You for guiding the properties to balance what is. Only the individual can achieve so much and then it passes along in its changed form to help others that now suit better. She needs strength\confidence of character to build confidence within that helps her be who she truly needs to be and that is just how it is, let it be what it needs to be…!!!

As I walk across the room inspiring, a presence of sexual, energy I see what attracts to me and vice versa. The elements in play thank me for today for today I bring you true unconditional love for all to see, once you lose that fantasy.

I was 16 with the wisdom of a 30 year old, so I was informed. I am now 33 with the knowledge of a 16 year old, as was to be. Join me in rolling back those years that we all try to turn back and see with new eyes.

The System

"The System" that charts itself adapts to what we need, what we are, and what we see. We build our framework of existence, mastering the elements to build a comfort zone, progression zone, development zone, fun zone…etc. There is one thing pure in me "Purity" to be sustained through all of it. Takeaway the physical forms and truly see. Stop the mind to truly think, sit, and just feel.

Adaptive systems with entire packages, layered as you develop further into and outer. We act, do, be, in the thick of it. Some come, some go and dismay, travel too, travel far, travel near, travel to travel and is all can be. Travel to get away, travel to be when just as you return you truly see.

Pick up pieces to put together and see what you see. Show the world who it is to be thee and seen. Magic and Mystery, the keys of form to believe what it is I be, showing a presence of existence to show it as should be. Stories told, people on hold, listening with sight, hearing that might, words are to communicate understanding of the conscious self to understand. We understand others but not words but feelings, inside, out. A language barrier show the struggle of translation within to become that person, educate with words of wisdom.

The conscious battle that you cannot win, do not want to give in. Just starting to consciously debate and fight an argument cause's anger in you. That you cannot consciously, see your manifesting at that moment. We live on the higher side of knowledge, knowing how we once were in its perfect and enhanced. Knowledge growing day by day of how to get back to it to fight it means it will win, to analyze it, it will win, to accept it and move through it and with it means no waves are caused for the friction to occur. Worst moments just carry you through not knowing how you really got there, until your there. Best moments are less though about what just happened, and then accept what it was that took you to where you are. We have knowledge to get through, our way with our understanding at that moment we understand we need to do. We choose to play with the words or the knowledge to consciously grasp what it is we are doing, have done, not doing.

The essence of it, is what it is, accept and move forward what next, what now, nothing, sit and wait, just be till it is time again to do.

Work, rest, and play in all elements of the whole day. You don't need to wait enjoy the work, rest while you're doing it and play with what needs to be achieved. Make yourself understand that the whole moment you are in. If disgusting is what you need to love and cherish doing it, it will not be until you absorb, truly before it passes onto another area to heal. Multi-tasking too much, love that you are able to Multi-task so many. It is a point of acceptance of your struggle, not aversion. Aversion is current in me to show my ways of addressing the moment. I bypass what is not comfortable with the comfortable; I fight my consciousness knowing I have my answer by the pattern I developed over time. Nobody is perfect; if they were, we would know and not exist like this. We exist together in the same pool of presence then nourish (or not) the earth and her ascension. Without limits, without gains we come to what she has (Earth) and take as much we need with no thanks. She will respond with here is some more…! So here's the weather, bright shiny day everyday through rain, snow, sleet, hurricane or storm coming your way I say Thank You for what I have taken this day for you to replenish this way.

If what we are a pawn as a star then I say that is what I can show this far. To the queen or rook there will always be pawns taken. Allow it to be in the cycle of things for me. Show the board for all to know the game it is that we are on show.

How much of what is free do you see? Not what the magazine is today but hey people believe the cost costs you nothing. To see something for nothing, no hook, no torment, no wallet, no seems on the edge of those dreams, the animals, the trees, the grass, the earth to be with limits of those monetary values, priceless.

Group and Universal

"Group and Universal Energies\Elements"

Group knowledge is very interesting where what is received, is received by all around, the form is similar when manifested through conscious forms and interestingly everyone receives the same but it takes hours, minutes, days before verbalised. People deal with the energies in different ways i.e. what comes to you, you feel, think, and express in multiple ways. This has happened with someone beside someone and me miles away. Time difference allows it to wave across the world. Imagine someone doing something similar as ourselves, thousands of miles away. What we cannot see does happen with similarities of the self.

New moon about to enter into a beginning, can feel it for days before the occurrence begins. 1427p today and I think around the 8th I knew adjustments are being made to welcome the change, now waiting in a lull to see the energies for the next few days brings about the enhancements to make.

Crystals are tingling with anticipation of what said, adjustment to be what is within me. Move the moments to be positive and not grim. Three days off a blast to see at last what was and has been the past, moving forward into the vast not holding the past.

About Me

"About Me" (In the physical)

33 Years old with a wisdom advancing in this reality I see. Born 24th March 1971 after the love energy of the sixties transpired giving Hope and Harmony to all that I see. Slept, slept, slept as a child bringing myself into the conscious physical realm, alive and playful, busy, and excited all the time. Schooling was a place to be to educate me, but did bunk off, not doing homework, not really listening and too many daydreams. Maths reports would show that I could not do the easy equations but could do the hard. Sport was my life, athletics, Football, Rugby, Martial Arts, Cricket, Swimming and Squash would be regular. Ran for miles each day in the way rather than walked.

Did some work as video delivery boy and cleaner at an airport? Took holidays at a caravan park where I was abused and changed my path to a more negative nature hating me and all around me. Nearly burnt down a school, by accident, got arrested for arson and taken to head mistress. Started building cars and wrecking them for banger racing, well I was the mechanic keeping the car running. Built a kit car, for racing around the streets, with expensive parts, got me into a lot of debt. Worked in the airline industry, started me drinking, and smoking through having fun and a good time, with little care in the world. Worked with Computers and Technology, left home began spending most of my time in work or in a pub, club. Drank all the time, finished off a half-full bottle of wine as I woke up for breakfast, then continued the day that way. Smoking drugs for a while feeling was great but out of it, looking for a release from working 100 hour weeks. Still to this day smoke and drink but nothing compared to previous days, women would come and go, couldn't hold onto a relationship, didn't want too, hated me and anyone close for no reason (I thought at the time). Late twenties I had travelled to 80% of Europe, Many states within USA, Central and South America and a variety of other place in the world, through working or holiday.

  Met hundreds of people, had been kind, generous, nasty, or hurtful. Would sit in a pub regularly; spend most of the salary in the bar. Buying drinks for anyone that talked to me. Remember I had 3 separate bar tabs in 3 separate pubs, 2 by work and the other near home, thought that was an achievement at that time. The flow of money and debt would just increase, was on a low wage, and spent 3 times as much on credit cards and store cards. Redundant after 7 years in a company, and had no idea what to do. Drank all night and woke with a younger woman, could not be that bad…! Started to look inwardly a lot from that point on, mortgage fell through sometime previously, drinking partner was sent off to drug and alcohol abuse hospital. I was lost and had to find work and somewhere to live soon, no money, no credit cards could be use anymore. Suicidal influences came, remember sitting in my flat with rubbish (beer cans, wine bottles, pizza's all around the room), with a knife on my wrist for hours, just not being able to make that final cut. I could not even do that. Started to pick up pieces after a long depressive state, found work that I wanted, began cleaning myself up (and the flat), had to move out, moved towards London away from where all this was, to leave it behind and create a new, working through as many issues that I could quickly do. I have now flittered around different companies, different industries as a contractor, moving locations every 6-12 months building a lot of money but still spending it on gadgets, drinks and smokes.

  Then one day not so long ago I had an amazing day. I remember it being a Saturday, I woke up for morning coffee and a smoke, sitting in the back garden for where I lived and somewhere from something inside blossomed, said Hello this is truly you what are you doing. I had an overwhelming warm and tingly feeling from the moment I sat outside in a bright sunshiny day. It was amazing could not wipe the smile off my face, what is this feeling; it is fantastic, like this.

  Went out for the evening, every man's dream was on its way. Women coming over to me 1, 2, 3 more than I cared to see, a promise that night to have sexual fantasies fulfilled with breakfast to follow eggs, bacon, sausages, the full English. I could not stop it, in the street all day, magnetizing beauty this way. Wanted to remember myself this way, slept alone that night (in dismay, drunk though) but the ramifications of my decision were correct this way. The search of others for the love they saw would not be very far. Changes had begun and I sensed a true meaning of the whole self as one. I to this day live a normal physical reality this way with the depth of insights and knowledge in the normality of both physical and spiritual to the last. A journey begins and has always been but needed to sin for the journey to gleam. Patterns created from the past adhered to, to work through and shared at last. The mistakes once made not forgotten, they excelled outwardly for all to choose to know, and not to be as was once demise in society.

Re-writing original ancient scripts to plain English for others to understand where there knowledge leads to, encompassed within, and to balance Humanity in Harmony adhering to purity, love, harmony and peace. Trusting in all that is and protecting against the negative transpirations within the group.

The group energy that comes through is global but it is a different mindset, realise that one thing means the same but different realities apply. It is difficult to foresee the foreseen I usually notice things before they occur, then realise after a change has taken place. As a tree branch hanging at eye level that could poke someone's eye out is then removed a few days later (for the good of humanity), the group energy picked up is that of others with thoughts of the same that manifest the change to happen. This occurs all the time with all that we see and do, unclouded by consciousness we begin to appreciate the potential within, from self, to the group, to the national, geographic, global and then duly universal. I can see what I do that makes changes from a few, to the many I sense with global intent. Issue's of feelings, fear, responsibility I hear have comfortably been met from past life's concerns and adjustments. The world needs to hear what it is that we sing clear. The wonders out there are right here for us to do and for us to share.

Balance between the two gives rise to a few, we deeply know how it is meant to go, that wonderful day to shine in the rays needed to show the harmonic balance for those. Different depths of reality and emotional turmoil are as hard as they need to be for the individual to see. A £100 debt means the same to someone as a £1 million debt to another. The feeling and changing process is the same based on an individual's pattern of existence.

Just as a tree knows all of itself and divine path we need to do the same, identify with the self to shine through all types of weather conditions to excel the unity process for purity and harmony for our mother use the energy you have to master the day as soon as you wake, work begins this way. As the seasons change and the stars too, watch and feel what is changing in what you do.

Bringing the self into the conscious self, many live in the consciousness of what they have always known, many find themselves into their inner self and sights. The balance between is what it will mean to be connected through a whole not just a made up reality. Whether you do or whether you don't it does not matter for which but both to broaden the knowledge in understanding the bad means to identify your route Spiritual and Man-Made processes and procedures. I know people that have chosen not to see their or follow their spiritual paths or insights but they still do follow the principles and I've watched them grow with only physical conscious knowledge and understanding to them they say so. I honour those that do, within them, to better their existence and hurting the few on the route that they follow but helping many more as they go. Watch the synchronicity begin, we resonate a vibration loud and clear for all around to feel and here watch as you start something and see how it comes back, connect the dots from this to that. Do not worry if at first you cannot see, the Taoist would say, "Just let it be". Overtime in just a moment, you will notice one, two, and then three and begin to watch what you do.

My path knowledgeable as it is also has to eat. I smoke and drink, as myself is required to give the relevant to receive insights required. There will be a time for these to end but not until this moment that I have fulfilled the trends. Accepting what and who I am as I am right now is a key element for balance inside you or me.

Very easy to get lost in the moment of doing, very easy to sit and judge what has been. Stability, protection, and grounding are true to one. The stability is fir the self, the protection is for interference that comes from negative and fluctuating of moment to throw off guard and the grounding to stay true and connected within which all balances together to hold back from sin. Pressure will mount and protection and focus need adjusting all for a moment to transfer what is within. Sending and receiving is only clear when messages are precise and simple for all manners to read and absorb the things inside, so begin to realise that the shell is to be protected so incoming alerts can be grounded to not be effective.

Today during the Day

Today during the day relaxed my own way chilled out until ready to be in presence of others apart from the girlfriend I see. Off to brothers to view the computer and see what is necessary to harmonise the functions and features. The computer being old needs updates and upgrades to fulfil future potential service to adhere to requests and demands of current physical realities. Data needing protecting, configuration and properties needing to be maintained to release the frustration of what once was a pain discovery of the whole was needed though, so not to lose what makes it whole. Refresh and replenish those elements within to once more rise and shine again. Computers emanate people in terms of properties, functions, and features they do what they know b force and commands of what is though. The properties in good and bad, positive and negative show what needs to show lets heal some of this on show? We mask in ourselves what represents in those components or resources that we use to give rise or ease of the whole we refuse.

Merlin of late is with me again to show the ways once known today. The layers within grow further than a grin. Global I see all things to be. There is much to radiate this day but balance it needs to be as we all must rise physically to see, the steps undertaken to climb and rise, watching and seeing through the clouds and trees. To understand the negative and positive is like an energy pole pulling from both sides with me in the middle as a gage to see when something changes in me. I could be happier this day but pull the wrong, the polarities and pressures must match to send the signals of balance to harmonise the track. The process will be complex on its journey to say but must maintain the physical balance this way. Body, Mind and Soul shows us all how it goes we need to consolidate what is this way within our pattern today.

The detail is clear, the premise is here, and the sky is blue as in the beauty of you. We are it every day from one to another this way. Closed user groups I say nay but expand that censorship to all this way. I have spent two years trying to be or back to the feeling I once was, shining so bright without fear or sight and now know it to be it is meant this way for me, we see things simply as right or wrong, we embellish them with creativity of conscious thought to say it is wrong. Trust in things set this way as they mean to be a test today, show and shine the true sublime and present this way that clothing today. The knowledge and magic we know can be overwhelming without guidance the master Merlyn is one of my teachers though, that I honour for helping me so.

Magic and mystery is not an individual art it is a conscious manifestation from the heart. True essence of creating generates from me to show the ancient writings for thee. A pot of gold is not what is dreamed but a reality so pure is the key. Though star signs we are shown the potential and properties though of larger things we all feel we know (and we do), they resonate deep within the soul of you. Tools of science once showed the way, through crystals and human souls this way, resonating truth not disguised and treated with open eyes. I hear people say it is a rock this way but we are too except we move with you. Adaptive and static outdated the presence to know in you, storage and knowledge is a clue of what is deep within the core of you.

Treat all aspects of this book in a reality but metaphorical, emblematic understanding of what resonates true with you. Some will say I hate this, this way; others be enlightened by what they see. It is a book I hear you say…! The true comes from you within with all your aspects in good or sin, take the foundation of what you read, feel and see and create yourself as you should be, in love, purity and harmony in mind when your consciousness goes into doubt and seething times. I am a practicing person just as you trying to excel that global view, working each day to resonate the balance of the whole this way, try it and see what becomes of thee. Take the global and universal understanding within thee. See what does work, see what does not, and believe in what you are free.

A book is only as good as the moment its read so receive this energy and knowledge and watch where you tread. The scope is huge; endless I see to become the whole of me. Friendly and nice, soft and gentle, Harmony and balance is not wrong or mental it is what you do already this way and want for you this very moment, this very day. Expand this out to all that you see and receive what is to be. Up days and down days are a presence to be accepting the reality is a wise one to see, we choose the moments to become a thing of the past, moving forward in my way at last. Helping others is good as it be but others to do excel the reality. This is not about obtaining what has needed, more so requested, truly within you to enhance your existence. The only thing you need to be aware of is how you resonate your existence out to others for them to feel, touch, see, and be and that's what is creating this reality overtime you see. An abundance that comes with it, in all the love, purity, and harmony that creates and watches what happens in and around you. All elements, all things, all ways, all days we generate a power not known of these days.

How others Transpire

How others transpire and see you through they and all too positive or negative to balance the whole. The book, the book, The Book to be a bible of me or is it...! This book written, fulfilling its journey back to a part of a whole human being or consciousness. Write, Write, Write I hear it so, the flow of things that are coming about, need to sustain clarify and purify of what this is be said. Tendencies to run off with words are frequent. Embellishing the simple that needs to say, clouding the consciousness, stay focused and connected, true.

The self with others, conflicts, united, passion, compassion, emotional, territorial all influence to test distraction and in balances, we work more each day with negative emotions and side-step ourselves in moments of address when all that's needed is for constant balance to stand true in what is within you. The interference from others around change the way you be today. Linking, Passing, Adjusting and working through what is in you. Support if support is from you, distance when distance is required. When relaxed don't choose what makes you relaxed, stay or be relaxed in all circumstances, be that self, kind and loving person, no need to use the words just resonate that existence within you and you will magnetize what is here for you. The answers are endless and always there consciously, spiritually they show and present you so. The matrix is set before you is so complex to give up now and then is ok to take a rest but stay in tune with the realities with you, live the life of many and see it through. Every moment in every way shines through each day. The notepad I write is easier one way than that, smooth on one side and the other not so flat but I flow with both to create a balance on the two to show these words through the paper onto you. I show you this day in a way the physical days present you this way. All encompass a balance but when the group shines through you will see another side of you.

I sit in a pub alone today surrounded by all this way, attracted to me is all that I see and attracted to them is where I begin. Emanating thyself for all to feel that balance and harmony. For them to excel finding words of calm, inside the fun, lifting those you can grimly see a surprise. The surroundings of me is full where the pub shows the rest as empty they come this way, this day unknowingly feeling properties of their day, will be good, will it be bad, will it be happy, or will it be sad. Only who knows what it is to be for them this day, they chose the chosen to prolong their current condition. With words of adjust and clarity that has needed to absorb the realities the self desires to be whole and happy.

Practical Mode

Practical Mode: A massive task was to be undertaken whereas to consolidate properties of machines into one. Being together smaller, older properties into a larger, more powerful one using more advanced technologies and knowledge than before. Full on work mode whereas uplift the change process to carry and refresh what is for a new day.

The build up is at first a discovery of what is and what needs to be, then a process of validating a move or migration to implement the process and verify existence of all functions, features and securities relevant thereafter is for what it needs to be for any remaining aspects to be healed.

Long hours took most my time adhering to make the transition seamless and addressing the problems before they arrive. My colleague and I were to partake in this exercise. His persona is do, regardless of consequences, mine to heal the process and problems, us to initiate a balance and understanding from what was to take place. I carried out all initial work and colleague fulfilled the assistance with speed for us to meet a weekend changeover.

We had over 30 tasks running at the Friday night to transfer their existence from old machines to the new. All tasks ran and completed successfully without problems. All data was now in the new that was set up as multiple processes using functions of advanced technology. The Saturday day was to verify all transfers completed successfully, old machines to be switched off and not be used then the sharing can begin to assign who and what requires access to and how on the new.

In first part, the old machines changed to restrict access to which they were uncomfortable with to change and we were mindful of problems they made. Addressing each with individual intent, they become present in their new environment.

We maintained a constant need for them for problems that could arise, as a fault tolerance device. Once all were where they should be all focus was from me towards the sharing of properties and securities. The rest of the weekend was a rolling change process to work through group energies of the change just made to bring properties of old connected from a new without changing the elements of the environment to view. Access granted based on who is who and what knowledge is required from each of you. Hundreds of people affected this way without a hindrance of being restricted on Monday.

My journey on Sunday into work redirected via an airport. To roam around with healing knowledge of change to pass on to anyone who came. An hour had passed to fulfil that task onto completing the task at last. The journey was short: Usually a bus near me would be, whereas today the service runs a Sunday, but not at this station. A walk required to the other end of town where another service at every hour I found. Missed that bus by a minute or two, took that as a sign for no bus this moment in time. As I walked through town to this bus stop, I felt a need to go into the train station and stop. Should have listened to save my feet finding out I missed another bus this morning. Headed back to the train station, this meant train to airport then another bus. The journey was quick as the distance was short and after the walk through the airport caught that other bus to work. Comfortable with all that is. Reach work to continue. All went well, just a procedure to follow to adhere to request for smooth transition tomorrow. During the weekend, I guided to see the areas that required attention from most, if not all from intent of me and so a little would come up the following day.

Monday arrived and early we went, off to work to see the events. Two problems arose that brought attention a person had access to old information. The frustration gone through for this person to be, as shouting the odds for healing to be, an angry, frustrated man who needed help not in a technical way. I sent the healing required for him as he requested unknowingly to him consciously. His physical problem immediately solved but the long-term effects of healing will come to him slowly, gradually when he is ready and he is not so cold.

He can choose to be what he is this day or take the opportunity for healing and change is his goal. Time will tell. The other problems was another for me that the process the same dimensionally. The person has hidden all that he has, being a secretive man, and not trusting in this or that. Healing sent once again to show the properties in such a way that he could lose all he has because of hiding things inside his way. All in all, the project complete relieving resource to be replenished and neat, to be sent off for healing a new in another site for those who need too.

10p Insight

10p Insight:

Did I know or manifest it so?

In the morning journey of the day, walking towards the bus stop the regular way, needing some fags and a 10 pence piece for the change, to the bus to lead me this way. Hoping my change will come at the shops, knowing I have a pound already got; fags I think are £4.9? (Something) usually change of six or seven, this day was £4.90 meaning what I got was the 10 pence change needed. The wonder in me is did I manifest it, the 10p I needed for my journey. The wise man inside tells me if, maybe I knew all along it would be and the rest was the conscious reality. Trusting in what it is to begin I let it be what it is for me.

The journey today sends help the child's way. I arrive at a train station and the ticket desk closed, I got to the machine "out of service" as seen, no ticket for my journey. I am on the train and no conductor the same; arrive at my stop and no collector to show. Yet I think of buying a ticket though. Using my instincts moving through my body and passed, then out of the station, a free journey at last. I enter the mall for shopping and I reach a woman with a charity box, I know the answer to my positive motion at last, my free journey was meant to be passed on to those who need it now so readily, and the group energy is balancing the positive. A pound I put and wondered after should it be the £1.80 for the train journey. The knowledge was the amount was correct with the addition of my positive energy sent along with it. The balance been made and what was meant to have been.

Money is a form of universal energy; I see a notion raising in me that for every pound 80 pence added from me in energy. I lend this 'Money' for it is not mine to be passed along and one day that will come back to replenish again this way to be carried for the positive this way.

I bought a large bag from a market stall £14.99 says it all, I advised do not worry about the penny change and was offered that I can leave the bag and have it looked after so I can go and do more shopping without worrying about carrying it around. Although I chose to decline the offer that penny was worth a pound! Soon after I paid for a pint £1.99 and did not advise to not worry about the penny change where I got the service and pint I asked for with no trimmings! It is a penny, just a penny!

Trust in the process with objects that be, that we hold precious to thee. I sit in a pub with all that I have purchased testing the group for a higher purpose. I say to me as I have done multiple times before leave all that I have today open to explore. They can take if they choose what I have bought maybe lose, but without my consent will come back to the accused. I leave the properties of this with all that I leave on the table or by my knees. The mobile, the bags, the other things too I have bought I am off to the bar without a second view. Waiting to be served I wondered if still there not turning round to look and see if I'm wrong, trust in those around you, you'll see and they will surprise yourself. I bought a pint and all is well so I think more time will tell, gone upstairs to the toilet to relieve, leaving behind those things or objects to be. Run out of smokes, to the vending machine I see and on return, everything still as it should be. I like to test myself in trust within the negative that we must. To work with the negative is to bring it alive and duly healed in the realm that is.

Shopping Centre

Shopping Centre:

The Anger, Frustration, Anxiety to name just three the shopping trip to change all of thee.

We are here as one taken what has been here to overcome those frustrations inside, the fear so alive, live and breathe it, and then decide. To move and work with energy that exists become that moment with those properties of the abyss. Raise them up until they are so pure and pass them round the factory floor. Help others see what you can do in and they will shine just as thee. The immensity of today is getting a bit grey as I balance my energy to handle this way; the group energy is strong, stronger than me they give me the protection to help this process seen.

Up early and it begins

1/ Grounding: Grounding to be strong, the local trees edging me on. They assist in connecting my whole to the earth to tap into the knowledge and properties for birth. Into those it will roam and go as intended and previously so.

2/ Me, Myself and I: Connecting to me. The whole presence connected with my whole reality the good, the bad, the negative and positive to guide a root through from anger, frustration, and fear within.

3/ Dimensions: All aspects of self and of that around connect with us and sign us around, about all that we feel and see this way 7 dimensions needed today.

4/ Universal: On the train and the vortex has come connecting me truly into one. Feeling the energies so vast and pure, the rainbow vortex is here to explore.

5/ Thoughts: Release all thoughts of the moment to adhere to true presence for the process here, releasing those eye-catching scenes and noises that cause reaction in me.

6/ Protection, Protection, Protection: I feel as the growth of connection spirals up the hill. The potency is strong and must move along to succeed in this way protecting all along.

Arrived at 1000a on my chair to begin and almost immediately its here, I sit in my chair in the physical here but dimensional aspects are becoming clear. 12ft above in the shape of a star, I rise to this moment to see this from afar. Emanating from within those properties to connect all humanity from the mind to spirit or head through the neck.

Overcoming those moments within them is a process the individuals mostly shelve. People look and some do stare, what is that they are looking at, I hear. The energy will last for a few days to come the 12:12 new moon will embed it into those ones. Their choice will also remain a 'free will', for them to gain.

Difficult to write as emotions in me deals with the elements in the group we see. They all are within the boundaries of the self and hope given with a pure energy ball from within.

Stronger and stronger I feel the need to protect continually as it continues. Energy is now a constant flow receiving from the above and below.

Many tables exist but they sit at tables next to me, what a wonderful feeling knowing they are tapping into this energy.

Layers of wave pulse from overhead from the dimension above the head. Present and bright an amazing sight as see, sense and feel the angels delight. Emanating now out from where we are to travel the world dimensionally. Both above and below the energy signature travels so. From above the waves come to the ground and from the core, it emanates out, meeting where humanity will be for the moment, they can carry and see. Time will tell how this helps those ones given a depth of knowledge in all their relevant sums.

Unicorns, Dolphins, Shamans and guides all coming to help this slide, apparent to see what is close to me to bring a balance through Love and pure harmony.

If I close my eyes, I see from a view, which is 12ft up in this physical room. Interesting to see how beauty becomes is part of all these frustrated, anxious ones. I'm here for you to give to you this way knowledge known from time of past, the future that will change at last, more important than those is the current we see, as that develops so much beauty in all to be.

As I write this way, my mobile usually turned off to say or messages stopped by others this way. I receive a message from one I love that states she is getting a cold, runny nose, headache too much. Between the lines she is addressing within what is being presented to begin, her start is notice of the physical ailments and what she chooses now will ride with her until an understanding is aloud.

People have come and it is so fast they sit down quick then gone before you know, picked up what's needed and off they go.

A few are staring knowing its morally wrong but cannot resist because of what is going on. I give you my energy, as it has to help you be whatever way you decide to pick from me. No need to look and stare but focus that presence over there, the physical guided through eyes, nose, and ears to connect with dimensionally feared. They'll carry today and build this up, raised it on and talk along to grasp what it is they know yet they consciously have chosen not to see so. It will come when they connect with themselves with higher intent and knowledge they have just shelved.

At 11 O'clock we are off round the town to pass as many people we can emanate, the world unified together to see, balancing together as we go between 11 & 12 for an hour or so!

If you stand in one place for a day, you have travelled the world, have you not (your energies have that you give and share with the good of all intentions). Knowledge, understanding globally gained in all that exists without language barriers in the way. When you help another times it by 10 to give ourselves an understanding of how many needed you then. Dealing with those properties helps others the same, connects with all exists this day. Healing the group energies first starts within, as we cannot aspire to know what to do consciously without that knowledge to begin.

See the world as is, in touch with feelings and senses, becoming whole, and together we make it known. A week has gone by lining up today with or from powerful beings this way. We walk tall and strong and can only deal with what is wrong. Every moment in every way needs the enlighten soul to travel the earth today.

Balancing and harmonising the world around you and in you today, never forgetting what was this about this way. For however high things can climb, the same said below does not shine. Choosing a process to climb high this way being comfortable with all to do and say balances thyself with an upward trend that has no place to ever end.

To discuss is to balance without the emotional turmoil with it sees a grasp of material or emotional gain, control! The teacher teaches the pupil but the pupil teaches the teacher. Allowing all aspects of he knows more or she knows less except the reality that both are best. In the exact moment with all properties to hand you will find both we are right to notice there hand. Excepting and trusting, incorporating into others discussion and views to you as its within you the balance needs to be that hasn't yet been consciously understood in thee. Their helping you see. Difficult I know in the moment though.

Through negativity received runs through and out in a vein to be to release through me in terms of the physical being.

A happy train conductor inspires a happy thought a warm welcome as he asks for tickets. Identifying a beautiful woman aloud in a way not to offend the young man, the partner to bring rise to the moment, without offending.

We aspire with things everyday to see things our way. To reach fundamental reasoning or understanding masters those properties in us and all around for help and guidance and then it expands once you've grasped your reality and sense of self it comes with knowledge received from given too others. Who you meet, who you see, who you think of, what you identify with, how you think of, what you identify with, how you identify with it....etc.

Through whatever we meet, we eat, we know, we go, we become what is the sum of ourselves as the moments unfold.

The presence of all that is has to be protected to see clearly the mastery of all that's to be, becoming the interface to pass through, receive, redirect, balance, hold or heal using resource of all that is, is to aspire through with majority of humanity. The weeks to come and weeks that have gone encompass a presence now, to foretell the old, present the new, and heal the moments that are ill will.

Changes a foot to know what is to be, manifesting purer realities. Creating mystical energies to balance the in between stands a foundation of growth.

Seeing things as they are, issue worked through, and patterns presented as truth, rather than fiction. Realities becoming present and on the highs to start the process again and again so what becomes is a comfort zone addressing all those areas of knowledge needed to gain or receive to change the presence of the interface from struggle to acceptance, hate through to love, re-programming the bad with good and negative with positive.

Entering into a negative, understanding its properties and bringing light, happiness educates the interface to knowledge of not bad or hurtful but a necessity to facilitate a need to address and heal. Bring light to all that comes and become comfortable in all that is. Stay balanced for the true harmony and others will feel and follow suit. Too far, too little hardly noticed, stand in the middle and let it be what it is.

In the next couple of years, comes what may, there are issue's to deal with every day. In every way feel them, associate them, and watch what they need to feed what they want and grow that knowledge to encompass all that connects from energies of a tree to a cat or dog. Wild animals to see, plants that become me, designs that insight me, sounds that excite me, sights that present me, smells that expel me and so on. Childs play; connect the dots to see the lots. Opportunities that come some are needed or maybe just one. Encompass all around that is needed to fulfil that process chosen by thee to become balanced and true with purity in you.

No fear – no hurt ride on through the dirty as it will change, to trust in a process that all wants to be the same aspirations I have in thee. The world will and is becoming but the truth exists within the knowing not only do we excel high we overcome realities of self creation, currently all that once was in me has nearly been relinquished back to the society. I have nothing and aspire this way that what comes in to deal with. Wisely and harmoniously, it comes and goes and nothing left to take a plunge.

Demise of the self and others comes through pattern of existence to relay or accept rather, that not to allow influence gives rise of an issue. Discussion and enhancement of digging deeper to understand the realm of the moment should only be forward with warmth influenced by negative increases the weight and depth of what is negative. Protect against and choose not to allow an influence push into you.

The woman that walks towards me stops and turns to head off. I feel she needs what knowledge and energies I have as she walks towards me. A big woman I see, beautiful is she. Allot of love inside to provide, yet she looks, notices and stops for a moment then turns and walks away. As it comes to me that, the potency is still strong she only needs that moment at that distance for her to move on, nothing more, nothing less, just enough to be and then agree.

Deeper Meaning

Understanding

Chart

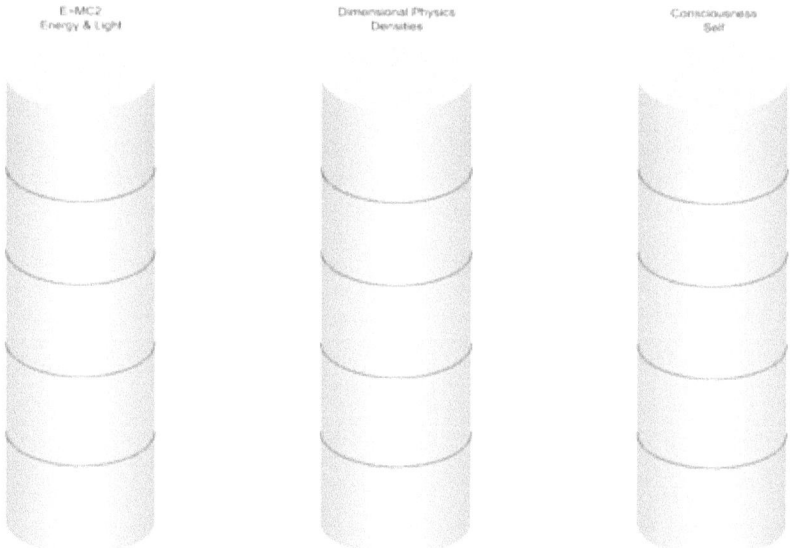

Self Understanding

Chart Meaning

Imagine the three cylinders overlapped together and the attributes of each therein. Look at an object and perceive the linear approach or view of it, the E=MC2 part it is what it is, as a static line. Include from there the understanding dimensionally or layers that energy filters through light and stops or clusters together at a point where the linear view is. The more energy to cluster together the denser in mass the object is.

Think about the object being you as human being, the reality you consciously relate to are the point where you sustain the energy to cluster together and form the density of you. Everything is dimensional so it's a matter of using tools or abilities to bring about greater understanding, starting from it is what it is known as, the reality of things. Which is also about accepting your reality or the objects as is. At this degree of density, there are loads of tools and written literature and studies to identify with all the physical aspects of the object or human being.

These are undeniable to the common reality of today. Whether it is right or wrong, it is a perceptional point of view or understanding. Physically we act or re-act to that degree of self-density so that cause and effect aligns with the densities in reality. There's more going on, allot more if you ask me but not in a normal sense because of depth of insight requires that you perceive differently depending on the depth of self as in dimensional self.

Example being; if you have a deep meaningful conversation with someone and there is during the conversation no relevancies of time (lose track of time, or meditative state) this would relate to a high 4th dimensional perception whereby time does not exist. If you perceive normality from this position of self, there is greater understanding of the object or self. It is in this regard that the position of perception becomes important, like seeing things from this point of view. You see things the same as in normal but also greater than as well.

Position of Consciousness

This document starts becoming a bit difficult to explain because what I'm trying to explain exists beyond the normal perception, so initially I would look at this and say don't understand it don't believe and I would be right, because I would be looking at it from a normal perception rather than a deeper perception.

Traversing these depths of perceptions, I find that it all relates in terms of mass flowing through light whereby the perceptions become denser in manner. Senses are lighter in resonance than emotional fields, emotional fields being lighter than thought forms, and thought forms being lighter than words or physical action.

The deeper you go within yourself the less density is apparent, so much so that words become obsolete, you actually find relating, where you choose a word for this or a word for that there are billions of relevancies in the resonance, of this or that. We have no words for a lot of resonances so words are like a brief or example of what we sense in ourselves, but our conscious focus being thoughts and words drives the energy through our sense's and emotions to become what we deem as apparent for use in our perceivable world, in line with densities of reality.

Relating this to $E=mc2$ whereby emotions are the matter, mass at a less dense form physical self. The energy created 5th dimensionally is to a degree of density for 5th dimensional reality, there from the densities created there to my thought forms of a 4th dimensional density or reality, degree of and duly onward to words or physical actions 3rd dimensionally.

Now, not trying to say that I know dimensional physics but I am aware of this process in me and can only relate it to dimensional physics, the difficulty is to explain it. Where I perceive words and physical actions as 3rd dimensional physics, changes when perceiving a reality of 4th dimensional physics, as is living a reality whereby everything has another depth of it that traverses to what we currently perceive as it is. Therefore, it is the same but also different, it is like understanding or knowing how it exists without seeing it.

All my life I have known more in regards to what I understand of something rather than how much understood. It is as if intelligence relates to how much in broadness of knowledge and this relates to both broadness and depth of knowledge.

Method

Everything that is perceivable comes from initially a depth of understanding, the more you inspire yourself to understand deeply about reality or relativities therein, and then the greater depth of understanding becomes a trend of growth to understand deeply. It is a cycle.

Energy feeds us all the time and the deeper you perceive relevancies within you the more neutral the energy is, fine, lighter more difficult to detect in changes or fluctuations. For me this is going on but people do not talk about it or relate to it. Therefore, I wondered for a while why and then just accepted that people do not find it relevant. I now conclude that maybe this understanding helps others understand.

If you perceive relevancies within you i.e.….give them focus and attention, you will progressively comprehend more and more at each moment, but the development is very slight so over months or years there would be more of a perception or awareness of meaning. The simply view is what you give conscious focus to becomes part of your conscious reality, regardless of density. The lighter or less dense your intention the lighter your perception will perceive. This also means that slight movements or attitudes within you become more apparent.

Flow

Energy traverses dimensionally like a filter where abundance of energy at its deeper relevance comes through in insights or senses. We use it to see how we have designed ourselves to be. To filter through into awareness, observations, perceptions, belief, emotions, and thoughts and outwardly as words or physical actions, making or adjusting external objects or internal objects as we go. Whole of ourselves and everything else is just energy in formation and we read and decipher just the surface of what it is to evolve that energy, either within us or external to us from us.

Anything created from a human being is just setting the energies in certain ways to fulfil the inner insight, idea, and belief as to what it should or wanted to be. Everything exists for the purpose of its existence and evolving its way. All energy has freewill of its own. The lighter or less dense the energy perceived traversing through us the more radiant the matter is, as it is less dense. Senses, emotions, thoughts, words, actions are just means of creativity like tools or systems to manifest the desired outcome whether it be matter visually seen or not.

Awareness is very important to understand what is happening with yourself so that you can identify with aspects or attributes of energy within you learning and understanding more relevancy or depth external to you. You and it are just energy and light the degree of density is to your own choice of comprehension.

Depth of Insight

Understanding Layers

Words against words are what we aspire yourselves consciously to align with, it is the density or depth of relevance of everything we consciously relate too. Physical self aligns with the conscious relevancies of matter.

Greater meaning to words or physical objects, our physical self comes from thoughts where thoughts related to thoughts inspire words or physical understanding.

Greater meaning to thoughts comes from our emotions, reality of emotions seeing the world and everything in or around us by means of emotions then consciously we interpret to thoughts of a denser degree. Because lighter influences occur, the deeper you go more broadness or understanding is gain by emotions than with thoughts.

Greater understanding and in line with planetary resonance's is our resonance or sense's, a reality to this degree is vast, learning everything in terms of vibrations or resonance greatly increases understanding of any given object or emotion or thought.

Key area or interpretation to understand is that if we think we create the density of what we think, if we feel we create the density of what feel. If we observe we understand what is apparent to know capacity we create. Allowing our senses to drive our understanding filter through, the lighter densities into our consciousness giving rise to lighter thoughts and feelings. As the objects are of lesser density more can be store or related to consciously at any one given moment, hence greater understanding can be gain by more energy of a lighter density, lighter thoughts, lighter emotions.

Consciousness's

Consciousness

Consciousness aligned with Reality, so shifting consciousness you need to give it a new focal point like perceive something deeper than it is.

Sub-Consciousness

Sub-Consciousness is the Trends and Cycles of thoughts or Realities so if you progressively do something it sustains the trend of thoughts of how to do this or that so to release the conscious load on doing it all the time.

Unconsciousness

This is holding the completed image or design so that all of your self is collaborated into the conscious vision of aspects or elements that you desire for your Realities.

Higher Consciousness

This is the global or group of energy influencing the individual to become greater or broader than before, it is the internet resource to the complete self-comprehension.

Dimensions

Words

Spoken words vibrate physically to sense or hear accordingly by vibrations in reality.

Thoughts

Thought forms influence the matter or physical words spoken so the calmer more neutral thoughts give less of a potent drive towards the words spoken or actions taken.

Emotions

This being our electro-magnetic hubs managing our energy fields from different aspects.

Vibrations

The Vibrational self resonates with the whole self, inspiring the emotional, to the thought, to the action or words manifested.

Instructions - Energy

Everything to the tiniest you can fathom is inclusive within the tiniest energy so all of everything is inclusive of all of everything, you change this, and this changes all. New instructions are inspiring and evolving life towards given directions by our creative self, all Vibrational, emotional, mindful actions are inclusive and manifested so we act them out accordingly. The more inline we are our energy the more we understand and flow with life.

Modules - Tools

Consciousness

Consciousness deciphers the aspects of reality and filters them into thoughts and duly emotional and vibratory elements. Like the management module for the individual's reality.

Forms

Creativeness of the individuals mind towards a Perceptional relevancy of energy or Vibrational or emotional into consciousness via methods of thoughts based on trends from life trends of thoughts consciously.

Feelings

Programme to identify with the emotional positions, movement, and potency of the emotional elements from our Vibrational energy fields.

Sense's

Vibrational elements of our whole self, adjusting to the dynamics of changes or evolution to align with all that is.

Insights

Being the deeper side of the conscious reality, you are in now. Realities being mostly live life emotionally then your insights are inspired from identifying the Vibrational aspects to adhere to, enhance, or heal the emotional positions from a broader or deeper aspect or dimension of the whole self.

Manifestations

Reality

What you define relevant or important in life becomes your reality. Dynamically adjusting all the time from everything you see, hear, think, feel, and resonate. Deepening and broadening your complete self-comprehension, deepens and broadens your insights to what is your individual reality.

Vision

The dream scope or framework your vision aligned with your reality. It is the progression forwards from the conscious point of your reality. To inspire the vision you work with your reality towards the vision. The deeper and more constant the vision the more work with reality will build towards it and faster, by interactions of actions and re-actions.

Resonance

Everything vibrates either physically or dimensionally, deeply. The resonance is the Vibrational aspects that you include and become what you deem as your whole self and interact with the whole of everything in the same way. Flowing with planetary vibrations allows your adjustments in life to flow with all life.

Abilities

Belief

Belief is manifested form Perception whereby the way you or others perceive it with constantly giving weight to it becomes your belief.

Perception

Perception manifested from your awareness, whereby the way you or others are aware of depth or broadness, it with constants is giving weight to it and becomes your perception.

Awareness

Scope or framework from the whole self's comprehension. The broader and deeper you are about yourself the broader and deeper you will see about everything that is with or around you.

Insights

The higher consciousness view of what or where you positioned best suit your individual needs.

Filtering

We filter by means of restricting or ignoring the aspects we do not perceive as relevant to our reality. The deeper and broader you are within yourself the less filtering goes on. We filter in this and filter out that so that energy streams can align with the vibrations, emotions, thoughts, or actions that are required for us in reality. The more you broaden or deepen by means of letting go of filters the more your will be aware of, perceive and believe. Giving a much broader and deeper understanding or knowledge of everything you see, think, hear, touch, and smell.

Influences

Scope or Framework

Scope of the routines everything that is Vibrational, emotional, thoughtful, and physical. If we only want to be aware of this much, we only become aware of this much and allow the rest to go along its merry way.

Awareness

We are only aware of what we have built up to be aware of in our reality. Changing our reality to become aware of everything allows us to filter through perception that is not necessary for the given task at the given moment.

Perception

We only perceive of what we are aware of in our reality. Changing our reality to become aware of everything allows the perception to perceive more of what it is aware of at any given moment.

Individual

Main activity goes towards the conscious reality we believe is relevant to evolve. Group activities or surroundings influence our whole self, which in turn is deciphered our way and duly brought through to the conscious reality of the self-belief.

Group

Influenced by the individual realities and actions of life, collaborated to become a more evolve group.

Society

Influenced by the group realities and actions of life, collaborated to become a more evolve society.

Culture

Influenced by the society realities and actions of life, collaborated to become a more evolve culture.

Religion

Influenced by the groups realities and actions of life, collaborated to become a more evolve religion.

Country

As above, the aspects of all become a governance of reality. The collaborated awareness from within shared out, then duly perceived and belied in each individuals direction.

Continent

Same again, the aspects of all countries become a governance of reality. The collaborated awareness from within shared out, then duly perceived and belied in each individuals direction.

Planet

Same again, the aspects of all continents become a governance of reality. The collaborated awareness from within shared out, then duly perceived and belied in each individuals direction.

Universe

Same again, the aspects of all within the planet become a governance of reality. The collaborated awareness from within shared out, then duly perceived and belied in each individuals direction.

Soul

Whole Self

Energy manifests through realms or dimensions as energy moves or positions it vibrates dimensionally to manifest the emotional fields which in turn manifests the thought forms and duly the conscious realities or physical forms, actions, re-actions, words. The conscious self is working with a small amount of the whole self continuously scanning and searching for the need of the moment emotionally, thoughtfully, or physically. The small amount is about 10-15 percent of the whole self whereby the unconscious looks after the Vibrational or emotionally relevancies to what you are not including in your conscious self for progression or evolution. The whole self is far greater, wider, broader, and deeper than perceived. As all of it is energy, the most part of the energy manifested is to form the self as the self is in the physical. This is to align with the responsibilities of physical reality or matter. Therefore, we are streaming dimensional energy from within our whole self all the time to become or adjust, to heal, or to create the beings we are. As do we so does everything else. Thinking in a way all of everything manifested in the same regard so you deepen your insights or reality within yourself, you perceive or become aware of these aspects within you within it. So an apple is just an apple but also more.

Consciousness

As goes your consciousness to self, grows its movements and desires and actions or re-actions into a collaborated consciousness, global consciousness.

Emotional

As goes your emotional self, grows its movements and desires and actions or re-actions into a collaborated emotional field.

Vibrational

As goes your Vibrational self, grows its movements and desires and actions or re-actions into a collaborated Vibrational grid.

Energy Grids and Instructions

The sum of all the parts, interact with an electro-magnetic grid system with the planet. As we inspire ourselves, influenced by what is inspired on the network, grid, or web. The grid system includes all life, energy from all of everything influenced by Universal adjustments, astrological alignments.

Individual

Influenced by in most part the grid system and duly managed individually by individual needs.

Group

Influenced by in most part the grid system and duly individually collaborated by groups.

Society

Influenced by in most part the grid system and duly individually collaborated by groups through to societies.

Culture

Influenced by in most part the grid system and duly individually collaborated by groups through to culture.

Country

Influenced by in most part the grid system and duly individually collaborated by groups through to countries.

Continent

Influenced by in most part the grid system and duly individually collaborated by groups through to continents.

Planet

Influenced by in most part the grid system and duly individually collaborated by groups through to the planet.

Universe

Influenced by in most part the grid system and duly individually collaborated by groups through to the universe.

Filtering Desires and Inspirations

Everything is influencing everything

The individual aspects within the self are influencing the individual aspects within the self of another. By the means of desire or inspiration for something to become greater than it is, in doing so learning off methods known or unknown.

The delivery system we use to do or act on something or for something coded in energy for all to see or know our flow of life in the reality density we choose then aligns with how it comes about to you. Everything is immediate, the manifestation procedure to filter through the densities of reality we hold true become the timescale of deliverance. So if we are all in alignment with the flow of the planet what come around, comes around immediately. The aspects of groups, societies, cultures, and us slow down (perception) the progress for conscious awareness.

We position ourselves accordingly through life movements meeting and talking and acting towards our visions of inner self-desires these aspects to come about. The deeper side of events gives those a faster interpretation, as their awareness is deeper dimensionally to pickup say vibrational aspects and comprehended to their consciousness their way. Highly evolved souls will know in an instant what it is necessary to do at any given moment due to full awareness and direction of self mostly known by knowing the whole self.

Working solely in the moment giving direction by insight or desire allows new instructions, energy to come in to adhere to or learn. Everything everywhere is apparently a learning curve or a training, teaching curve. Whereby you can learn off this as much as you can teach this, due to the nature of each individual element is their individual nature, hence appreciating the elements as they are and working with depth of perception to increase or evolve forward. We do this every day in every way even when we say it does or does not.

Dimensional Comprehension

We know and work with constantly the comprehension of reality in 2 dimensional state, Yes, No, Right, Wrong, This, that. Two sides of the equation. The 3 dimensional comprehensions becomes apparent when using almost yes, almost no, 180 degrees right, 45 degrees wrong, being a polarity or static realm must align to the 2 dimensional sense of right or wrong. 4 dimensional comprehension is where your emotions are part thereof the same thing but different. The yes or no comes from almost yes or almost no and duly comes from the emotional depth included within. Difficult to put into words but imagine a sphere and the almost yes is representative of a sphere entering your whole self and it is aligned to some degree of matching your whole self. The almost being something like 270 degrees of the sphere is compatible.

Duly the 5 dimensional aspects will be the additional resonance of whereby all the emotional compatibilities are resonant with you. Each stage is greater, broader, and deeper than the last. So if you are just Vibrational with emotional or thoughts or words you are answering by means of sensing your resonance and reply with Vibrational resonance, like a sonar. But we are not trained enough to know all the relevancies of resonance's to communicate and sustain a workable reality, hence the reality we are in. took thousands of years to build what has been built with your comprehensions of realities. Now the planet resonating different tune, in direction, which is why we are continuing an evolutionary change towards our inner self rather than denser Vibrational reality. However, that being said we are also following our own trends of how we used to go about things towards denser aspects of acting or re-acting.

I cannot know everything about everything but I can tell you everything about me and my whole self who is intertwining with all and all self is in the Universe. Therefore, what vibrates vibrate with me and duly I decipher and manifest it my way with my trends towards a collaborate view into a density to be aired and shared. This is my perception, my understanding, my knowledge comprehended but I give weight to increase awareness, perception and belief of all things unconditionally from a neutral point or position which enables me to see and know for growth and sharing of knowledge for all and others to grow by inspiration or depth of perception.

The more I let go of self-belief, self-perception, and self-awareness the more I see of group or global awareness or perception or belief. Albeit a natural lifestyle instead of choosing this way or that I choose to flow with nature as thy self and grow by means of inspiring the essence of all I see without managing it to allow it to become what it is greater than before, purer than before by means of trends and constants. Maintaining a vision of universal peace and tranquillity, which works for me too, so it is a self-desire inspiring outwardly to groups to share. This includes all that is known and unknown, orthodox or unorthodox, and filtered through in a neutral comprehension.

There are thousands of diagrams or systems here are a few systems.

Diagram 01 – Consciousness

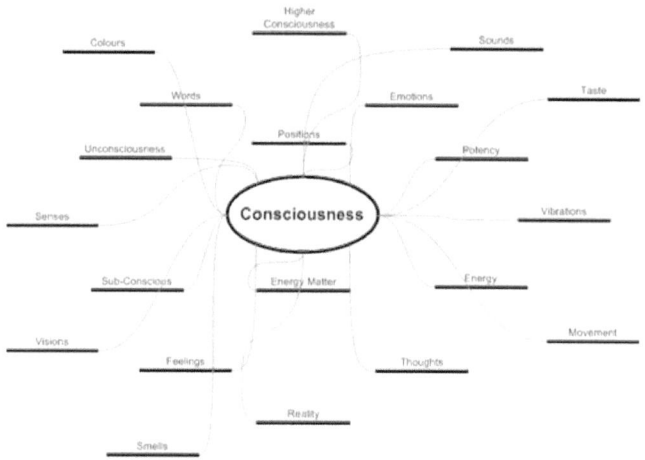

Brief of Diagram 01

Comprehension of Consciousness

- Higher Consciousness
    - Hub for interaction to influences external to self awareness
- Colours
    - Relevancy of Vibrational attributes
- Sounds
    - Vibrational environment
- Words
    - Matter manifested from thoughts
- Emotions
    - Matter manifested from vibrations
- Taste
    - Physical interaction through internal awareness
- Unconsciousness
    - Containment and awareness of whole self knowledge
- Positions
    - The insightful energy types and positions
- Potency
    - Strength of this and that
- Senses
    - Resonance connections to and fro
- Vibrations
    - Instructions from energy movements
- Sub-conscious
    - Automated processes and trends, this life and previous
- Energy Matter
    - The process from instruction to reality density
- Energy
    - Types and properties
- Visions
    - Imagery of given realities and scopes
- Movement
    - Energy positioning
- Feelings
    - Emotional adjustments, actions or re-actions
- Thoughts
    - Creativity of given attributes or awareness of from self
- Reality

        - The constant working environment of matter stream
- Smells
    - Attributes of energy awareness for aromas

Diagram 02 – Unconsciousness

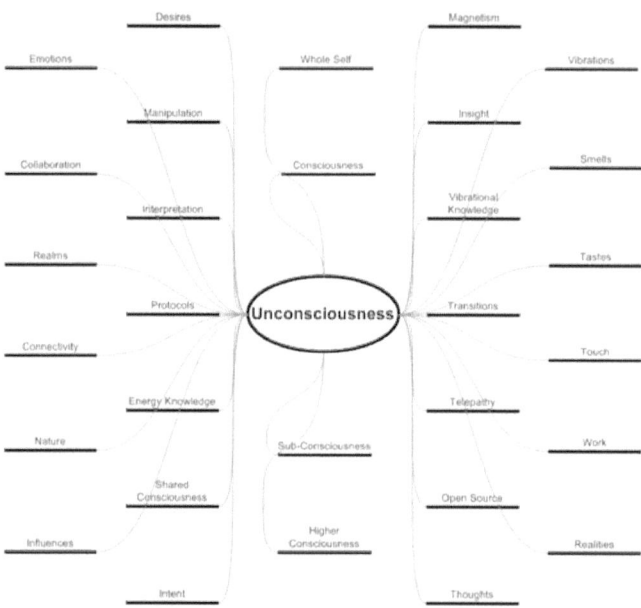

Brief of Diagram 02

Comprehension of Unconsciousness

- Desires
    - The collaborated view of what is current in your whole self and self reality awareness to adjust your intent
- Magnetism
    - Attracting the necessary of whole self imagery needs or desires
- Emotions
    - The whole emotional picture and depth of insights
- Whole Self
    - The management utility to filter through adjustments to whole self and present whole self with every movement

- Vibrations
  - The resonance of the whole self
- Manipulation
  - Energy needed or not comes to your whole self, filtering through your own perception of protected self. The more you sustain your own whole self image the more you are protected by means of knowing this is or not you
- Insight
  - The depth and dynamics of your reality insights
- Collaboration
  - The elements within combined and attached to your reality intent
- Consciousness
  - Feed and monitor the energy movements or adjustments to aligned with whole self presence
- Smells
  - Intuitionally expanding the smells depth and positional relevance
- Interpretation
  - The management utility to self's interpretation
- Vibrational / Knowledge
  - Bridging higher consciousness attributes to sub-consciousness filters to align with conscious reality means
- Realms
  - Multi-dimensional
- Tastes
  - Intuitionally expanding the tastes depth and positional relevance
- Protocols
  - Common transfer languages i.e. types of energies aligned with
- Transitions
  - The module of incoming or outgoing to or from the whole self
- Connectivity
  - Bridging the whole self to another object, person, vision
- Touch
  - Intuitionally expanding the touch senses depth and positional relevance
- Energy Knowledge
  - Storage or cache of whole self knowledge of soul
- Telepathy
  - The device for communicating whole self aspects
- Nature
  - Intuitionally expanding or aligning the natural needs or means for whole self containment

- Sub-Consciousness
    - Leading off of the unconscious instructions and feeding reality processes
- Work
    - The territory to drive things constantly duly wanting or not wanting to do by conscious reality means
- Shared Consciousness
    - The hub as whole self's presence in global sphere's
- Open Source
    - Unconditional comprehension
- Influences
    - All and everything at multi-dimensional layers
- Higher Consciousness
    - The governor or influencer of whole self, unconditionally
- Realities
    - Act in part 10-20% of the relevancy of unconscious self presence, the more realities your can perceive the more understanding and knowledge you can comprehend, broadness and depth
- Intent
    - Sustaining the needs and desires of individual self and duly the external relevancies and aspects necessary for self evolvement
- Thoughts
    - Where your thoughts are coming from or picking up relevancy, you choose everything about you in every situation in any way

Diagram 03 – Higher Consciousness

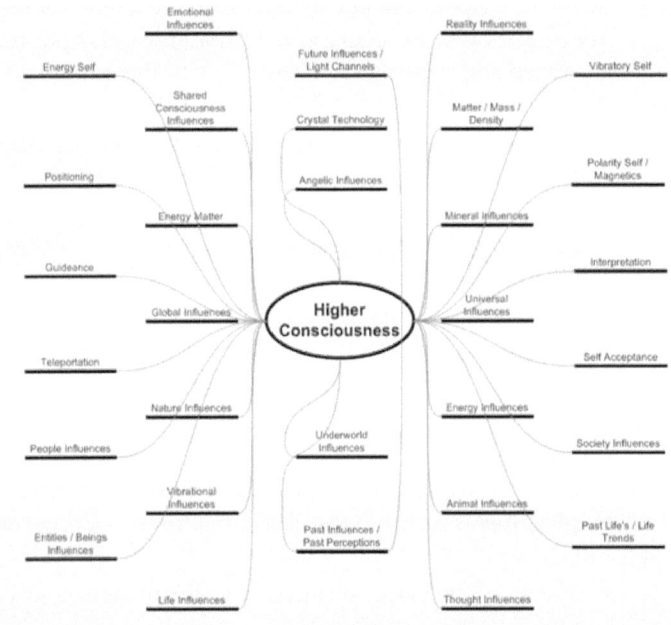

Brief of Diagram 03

Comprehension of Higher Consciousness

- Emotional Influences
    - Aspects emotionally of deep insights from Universal or global attributes
- Reality Influences
    - Energy feed towards changing or adjusting the current reality or understanding or knowledge
- Energy Self
    - The whole self influence on everything else towards global goals
- Future Influences / Light Channels
    - Inclusion of outer visions, broader or deeper
- Vibratory Self
    - Influences of planetary or universal vibrations
- Shared Consciousness Influences
    - Global attributes of insights and intents mostly external to self, how you fit in the world

- Crystal Technology
    - Resonance of advanced technological system purely streaming help and support and knowledge from the whole for self interpretation or influence as is technology today but much more advanced and dynamically changing with the moment
- Matter / Mass / Density
    - Combination and presentation of how we have manifested or forms functions, procedures in our direction of reality
- Positioning
    - Alignment with self and planets, universe
- Angelic Influences
    - The higher Vibrational resonance of possible self
- Polarity Self / Magnetics
    - What we attract or push and pull exist in reality towards higher self ideals
- Energy Matter
    - The flow of trends and constants from external sources to bring in adjustments or magnetise self needs to be delivered to reality
- Mineral Influences
    - Elements of the planet resonate with the planets model of itself and we duly resonate with
- Guidance
    - The assistance of elements or influences to support the changes of insights to change or adjust relevancies
- Interpretation
    - The comprehension of what comes in to work with in alignment with conscious reality
- Global Influences
    - Understanding or knowledge growth or evolution expanding the view
- Universal Influences
    - Understanding or knowledge growth or evolution expanding the view
- Teleportation
    - The movement in terms of energy self from location to location disengaging the physical matter and re-presenting elsewhere in a dimensional sense
- Self Acceptance
    - Neutral of mind to all things
- Nature Influences

- The natural afflictions of the elements of the planet, helpful, supportive
- Energy Influences
  - The construct part of energy coming in to align with the needs and support towards given goals or desires of self image
- People Influences
  - The bridging or connecting of the whole self resonance, filtering the comprehension through dimensional self
- Underworld Influences
  - The internal or inner world of planetary energy movement or adjustment and directions, trends and constants bridging earthly comprehensions
- Society Influences
  - The whole self directions for all in society group
- Vibrational Influences
  - Higher Vibrational relevance to the known Vibrational resonance
- Animal Influences
  - The movement or functions or adjustments meeting criteria of reality or physical self process
- Entities / Beings Influences
  - All known or unknown entities or beings are therein part of the same as we are the evolutionary growth in our individual direction in different layers of dimensional comprehensions
- Past Influences / Past Perceptions
  - Past influences from within own souls energy trends and others (people, planet, universe, animals, trees) at any degree
- Past Life's / Life Trends
  - Your own souls energies and influences building and developing towards the evolutionary alignment
- Life Influences
  - The reality of self's imagery becoming part of all the sum of all the parts
- Thought Influences
  - The mind set and belief towards self awareness, understanding, movement, growth, adjustments….etc

Diagram 04 – Emotions

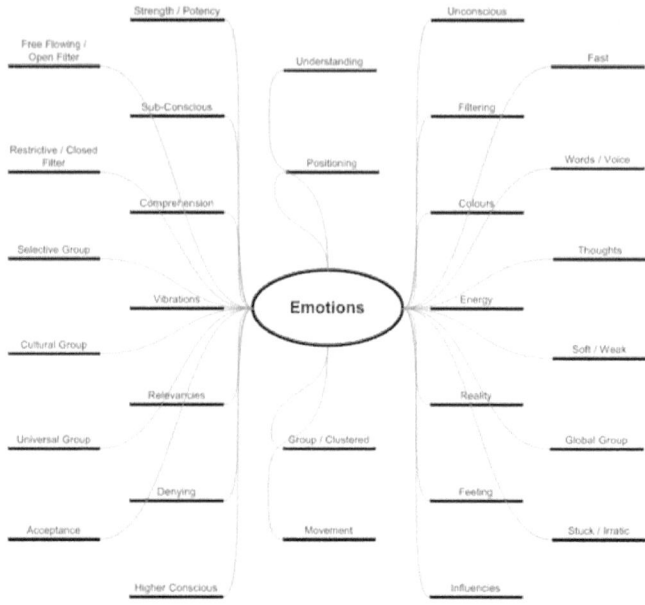

Brief of Diagram 04

Comprehension of Emotions

- Strength / Potency
    - The current aspect that is feeding the thought or type of thought
- Unconscious
    - What needs to come through or be addressed to move forward
- Free Flowing / Open Filter
    - Full identification of emotions without denial or potency increase
- Understanding
    - The comprehension of emotional self
- Fast
    - Speed of emotional relevancy on given thought
- Sub-Conscious
    - Regular or constant presentation of emotion
- Filtering
    - Feeling the whole emotion move or adjust in given moments
- Restrictive / Closed Filter

- o   Without conscious comprehension
- Positioning
    - o   The combined aspects of feelings towards an awareness or perception or belief
- Words / Voice
    - o   Behind the words are carried the thoughts, behind the thoughts the emotions
- Selective Group
    - o   Choosing the emotional relevancy of the thought
- Comprehension
    - o   Identification in part of the feeling
- Colours
    - o   Visual comprehension of feelings
- Thoughts
    - o   The feeling moods and actions or interactions
- Vibrations
    - o   The resonance behind the emotion
- Energy
    - o   The instructions within, how it operates, feeling your way
- Cultural Group
    - o   Collaborate feelings or emotions in a group
- Soft / Weak
    - o   Low resonance or fine emotions
- Relevancies
    - o   Connectivity of emotions to this and that
- Reality
    - o   The reality of self's portrayal in emotional views
- Universal Group
    - o   The universal influences to the emotional self
- Group / Clustered
    - o   Combined intent of potency or passion towards
- Global Group
    - o   The planetary combined emotional relevancies of all things
- Denying
    - o   Choosing to not consciously be aware of the emotional relevance
- Feeling
    - o   The alignment module or bridge to read and decipher in thoughts
- Acceptance
    - o   Emotions like thoughts are what they are
- Movement
    - o   Changes in emotional situations

- Stuck / Erratic
  - Blockage or bottleneck
- Higher Conscious
  - Influences of evolving the emotion
- Influences
  - Everything aware of, known or unknown

Diagram 05 – Senses

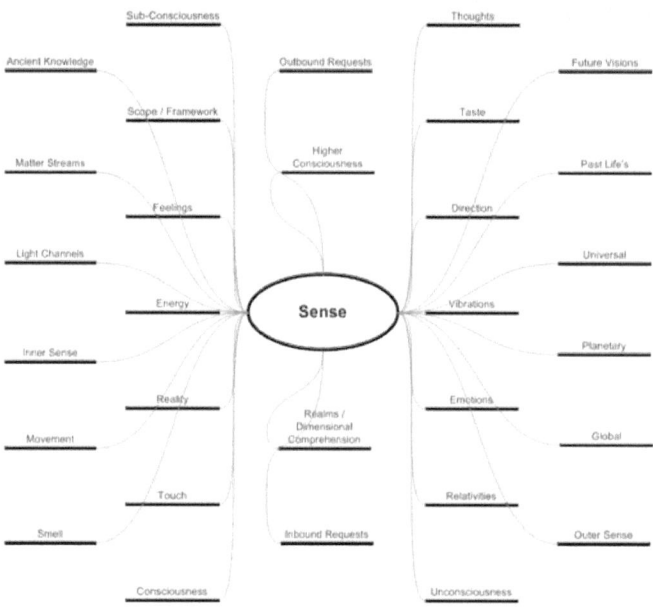

Brief of Diagram 05

Comprehension of Sense

- Sub-Consciousness
  - Observation of resonance of trends things that link in sense not thought
- Thoughts
  - The resonance of delivery of thought
- Ancient Knowledge

-
  - Explainable and comprehensible by means of Vibrational relevancies to all things
- Outbound Requests
  - Like a sonar wave delivering vibrations from whole self
- Future Visions
  - The presence or resonance of whole image
- Scope / Framework
  - Unconditional, universally wide, restriction by self belief
- Taste
  - Physical interpretation f vibrations of taste
- Matter Streams
  - The flow of constant vibrations and trends strong and light
- Higher Consciousness
  - Alignment module to sustain Vibrational self
- Past Life's
  - Vibrational aspects or functions or procedure, needs to do before moving forward or overcoming
- Feelings
  - The resonance behind the feelings and emotions
- Direction
  - Desire and intent
- Light Channels
  - Directional resonance
- Universal
  - Foundation of all Vibrational relevancies
- Energy
  - Instructions for movements to sustain Vibrational realms
- Vibrations
  - Waves of this and that
- Inner Sense
  - Sensing the ways or functions or procedures from point of view of sense
- Planetary
  - Earthly harmonics
- Reality
  - Sounds and music
- Emotions
  - Manifestation of vibrations
- Movement
  - Positioning of senses changing or adjusting
- Realms / Dimensional Comprehension

- - o Comprehension of physics of each dimensional interpretation of vibrations
- Touch
  - o Connectivity with physical attributes
- Relativities
  - o All of everything
- Smell
  - o Nasal channels
- Inbound Requests
  - o Sensing resonance of something, someone, nothing
- Outer Sense
  - o Aspects of sensing something is up
- Consciousness
  - o Real time interpretation of managing the sense
- Unconsciousness
  - o Whole self integration or awareness or adjustment of resonance

Diagram 06 – Reality

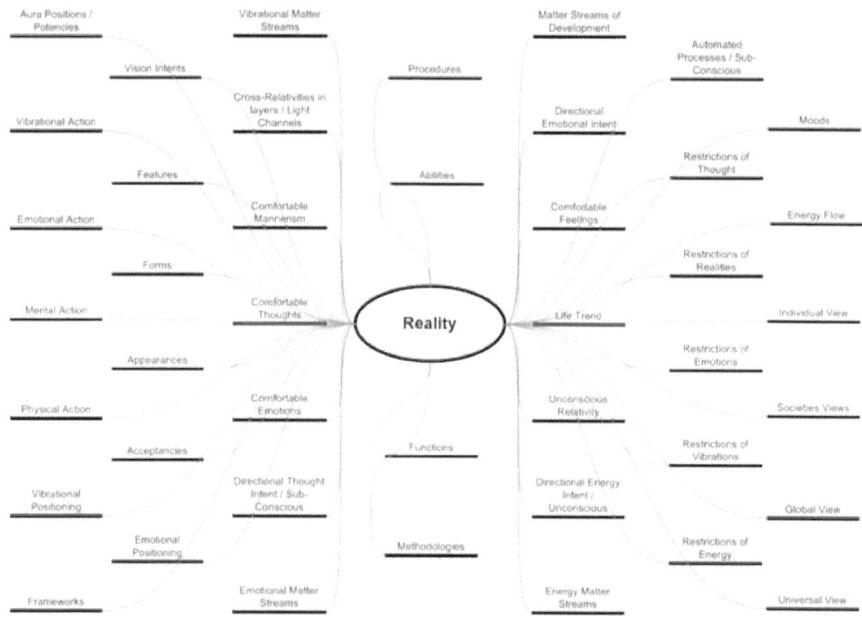

Brief of Diagram 06

Comprehension of Reality

- Aura Positions / Potencies
    - The whole self alignment with the energies of current reality or framework
- Vibrational Matter Streams
    - The resonance of everything
- Matter Streams of Development
    - Different matter streams of tasks to assist in evolution
- Vision Intents
    - Visionary quests of wholly seeing the sum of all parts in an image related to self conscious knowledge
- Procedures
    - How the object in realities is
- Automated Process's / Sub-Conscious
    - How the aspects of follow trends or constants
- Vibrational Action
    - Sensing the adjustments something is making
- Cross-Relativities in Layers / Light Channels
    - Insights and instinctual awareness of given directions of reality
- Directional Emotional Intent
    - The evolutional stance on emotional fields of self
- Moods
    - Emotional reality
- Features
    - The self's aspects in reality
- Abilities
    - The way or resources available for working with present moment
- Restrictions of Thought
    - Denials or karma
- Emotional Action
    - Movement or adjustment of emotions based on direction of intent
- Comfortable Mannerism
    - The acceptances of Vibrational, emotional, thoughtful, physical patterns or positions of self
- Comfortable Feelings
    - The acceptance of emotional positions of self
- Energy Flow

- o   The trends and cycles of all aspects
- Forms
    - o   Shapes, artwork, pictures, life, nature, animals
- Restrictions of Realities
    - o   Dis-belief of this and that
- Mental Action
    - o   The conscious re-action or action, intent
- Comfortable Thoughts
    - o   No re-action or action mentally
- Life Trend
    - o   Combination of all the parts within and the directions they are taking
- Individual View
    - o   Your take on everything relevant to your reality or not
- Appearances
    - o   Presentation, marketing, sales of self image
- Restrictions of Emotions
    - o   Blockages or bottlenecks present in your reality, denied emotions…
- Physical Action
    - o   Your physical movements, mannerism, or action
- Comfortable Emotions
    - o   The acceptance and awareness of the self's emotional stance on this or that, feeling angry without anger become potently or pressured in you
- Unconscious Relativity
    - o   The whole self's reality combining the aspects of conscious reality with the other aspects of self
- Societies Views
    - o   Your take and societies take on your reality
- Acceptances
    - o   Acceptance of the Universe as is
- Functions
    - o   How something works
- Restrictions of Vibrations
    - o   The blockages or caching of Vibrational relativity of self's functions, the flow of
- Vibrational Positioning
    - o   The resonance pathway and current situation or intent or delivery progress
- Directional Thought Intent / Sub-Conscious

- o How you perceive this will be in your reality
- Directional Energy Intent / Unconscious
  - o The passion of your self from your reality inclusive of the other parts of self
- Global View
  - o Appreciation and respect for what is and working with your whole self
- Emotional Positioning
  - o The current state of emotions
- Methodologies
  - o How you perceive things needs to be done
- Restrictions of Energy
  - o Denial of incoming energies to whole to work for your desire
- Frameworks
  - o The area you set with your scope of observation or awareness
- Emotional Matter Streams
  - o Manifestation from Vibrational aspects to form and adjust emotional aspects to flow to thoughts and words
- Energy Matter Streams
  - o The energy to filter through all dimensional plains and work towards a whole oneness comprehension in everything
- Universal View
  - o The awareness and observations in depth of insights of everything that exists

Insights - Future Being

       The potential of a human being to become greater than he or she is just unlimited. Because anything you can create mentally has its place amongst an entire universe of possibilities, the restrictions are of global proportions whereby the perceived physics make a lot of potential impossible in a denser environment or dimension. Believe in everything and everything becomes believable, know everything and everything becomes knowing, understand everything and understanding becomes everything.

       It is not about what we do but how we exist in the next few hundred years that will allow changes into objects and societies to take a footing. The efforts about something being less harmful are obvious in not harming but not delivering an understanding to how to be less harmful, meaning there will always be harm. The same with peace, peace has no restrictions it is just peace. You cannot apply restrictions to something that has none. In doing so you create rules and restrictions, which by itself defines, peace then comes about by segmenting or police people. Being in a peaceful state, you know that peace cannot harm, as you would not be capable of physically harming someone else from that state. No rule or restriction is necessary when self-awareness is at a place of understanding beyond the rule or restriction.

       Everything that you can be is relevant to how everyone can be; as you work on yourself and influence others, you inspire the same for other people. Their own choice to feel what you feel or sense how you sense will go about it in their understanding currently. The essence of being human is just that being human, but the complexities of how you are human right now are incredible. Understand your complexities and everything else will become easier.

What we notice about ourselves will change progressively; content of discussions will remain similar but less word used to give understanding and less of a defined response will be present. Mannerisms and attitudes will lighten as people identify more changes within them, than external to them. Greater understanding will come from individual words used as people appreciate more the thoughts, emotions and senses within the words. Physical actions will reduce their harmfulness of intent. Words used more efficiently and less harmfully as more understanding that is conscious comes about through thoughts, emotions, and senses. Thoughts will become lighter and less intense as less physical actions are necessary and more focus on emotions and senses. Emotions are much more relevant or potent than they are currently but not as dense or thick. Senses will become more knowing and relevant. People's resonance, their vibrations will be more noticeable, radiating.

www.ingramcontent.com/pod-product-compliance
Ingram Content Group UK Ltd.
Pitfield, Milton Keynes, MK11 3LW, UK
UKHW041436180426
11947UKWH00007B/467